Oxford
Children's

OXFORD
UNIVERSITY PRESS

Great Clarendon Street, Oxford OX2 6DP

Oxford University Press is a department of the University of Oxford.
It furthers the University's objective of excellence in research, scholarships,
and education by publishing worldwide in

Oxford New York

Athens Auckland Bangkok Bogotá Buenos Aires Cape Town
Chennai Dar es Salaam Delhi Florence Hong Kong Istanbul Karachi
Kolkata Kuala Lumpur Madrid Melbourne Mexico City Mumbai Nairobi
Paris São Paulo Shanghai Singapore Taipei Tokyo Toronto Warsaw
with associated companies in Berlin Ibadan

Oxford is a registered trade mark of Oxford University Press
in the UK and in certain other countries

This book was originally published as The Oxford Illustrated Junior Dictionary 1990

Compiled by Rosemary Sansome and Dee Reid
Illustrated by Barry Rowe

British Library Cataloguing in Publication Data
Data available

Paperback ISBN 0 19 910674 6
Hardback ISBN 0 19 910285 6

2 4 6 8 10 9 7 5 3

Printed in China

How to use your
Oxford Children's Colour Dictionary

To help you find your way around this dictionary,
we've made it very easy to use:

a b c d e f g h i j k l m n o p q r s t u v w x y z

- The alphabet is printed at the top of each page, with the first letter of all the words on the page highlighted in RED

- When you want to look up a word it is also printed in RED so it is easy to find.

- Once you have found the word you are looking for, you will see a clear definition of what the word means.

- Very often you will also find an example phrase or sentence to show you how to use the word correctly.

clock a machine that shows you what time it is

- All through the dictionary you will see lots of colourful pictures which are fun to look at, and which will help you to understand and remember words.

Picture Section

At the back of the book is a special picture section which contains many colourful illustrations of everyday objects. For example, you will find here pictures of thirteen different kinds of trees, eight kinds of dogs, twenty-two different flowers and plants, as well as sixteen major musical instruments.

A a

abbey **1** a big, old church once used by monks or nuns   *Westminster Abbey*
2 a place where monks or nuns live and work

abbey 1

abbreviation a short way of writing a word or a group of words. P.T.O. is an abbreviation for *please turn over*.

ability the power to do something *He has the ability to speak six languages.*

able having the power to do something   *She is able to sing high notes.*

aboard on or onto a ship, bus, train, or aeroplane   *All aboard!*

about **1** almost   *It's about four o'clock.*
2 that tells you something *a book about ships*
3 in any direction   *rushing about*

above **1** overhead   *the sky above*
2 higher than   *The aeroplane flew above the clouds.*

abroad in another country *a holiday abroad*

abrupt sudden

absent not in a place   *absent from school*

accelerator one of the pedals in a car. The driver presses it with his foot to make the car go faster.

accent the way people say their words   *Australians have a different accent from Americans.*

accept to take what is offered to you

accident **1** something bad that happens and is not meant to happen *He broke his leg in a bicycle accident.*
2 *by accident* by chance *We met by accident.*

accompany **1** to go with someone *He accompanied her on the journey to Paris.*
2 to play the piano or guitar while someone sings or dances

account **1** a story about something that has happened   *There was an account of the football match in the local paper.*
2 a list that tells you how much money you owe or have spent *a bank account*

accurate correct and exact

accuse to say that someone has done something wrong   *The policeman accused him of stealing the car.*

ace a card used in a game, marked to show it is number one. A pack of cards has four aces in it.

ache to have a pain that goes on hurting   *My head is aching.*

achievement something difficult or special that you have done   *Winning the medal was a great achievement for Jim.*

acid a kind of liquid that can burn your skin. Lemons contain a very weak acid.

acorn the nut of an oak tree

acrobat someone who does exciting jumping and balancing tricks to entertain people

acrobat

across from one side to the other
I swam across the river.

act **1** to take part in a play
2 to do something *The girl acted quickly and was able to save the drowning man.*

action **1** doing something
2 something that is done

active busy or working

activity **1** an action or occupation.
2 something for you to do *The sports activities on offer at school include netball and football.*

actor a man who acts in a play

actress a woman who acts in a play

actual real

add **1** to put with something else to make it bigger *Add another brick to the tower.*
2 to find the answer to a sum like this $3 + 3 =$

adder a small snake with poisonous teeth

addition **1** adding numbers
2 something that is added *The addition of the curtains made the room much brighter.*

additional extra

address the number of the house and the names of the street and town where someone lives

adjective any word that tells you what someone or something is like *Beautiful, tall, nasty, delicious,* and *difficult* are all adjectives.

admiral a very important officer in the navy

admire **1** to think someone or something is very good *The teacher admired his work.*
2 to look at something and enjoy it *They were admiring the view.*

admission the cost of being allowed to go in.

admit **1** to let someone come in *No child under ten years of age can be admitted.*
2 to say you were the person who did something wrong *He admitted that he stole the jewels.*

adopt to take someone into your family as your own child

adore to like very much

adult someone who is fully grown

advance to move forward

advantage something that helps you to do better than other people *an unfair advantage*

adventure something exciting that happens to you

adder

adverb any word that tells you how, when, or where something happens *Away, often, somewhere, now, slowly,* and *quickly* are all adverbs.

advertisements words or pictures that try to make you buy something

advice what is said to someone to help them decide what to do *My advice is save your money.*

advise to tell someone what you think it would be best for them to do *The doctor advised the girl to rest.*

aerial

aerial wires or metal rods for picking up or sending out radio and television programmes

aeroplane a flying machine with wings and an engine

aeroplane

affect to make someone or something different in some way *Her handwriting was affected by her sore finger.*

affection the feeling you have for someone or something you like a lot *Most children have a great affection for their pets.*

afford to have enough money to pay for something

afraid frightened

after **1** later than *You finished after me.*
2 following *Dad went to sleep after dinner.*

afternoon the time from the middle of the day until about six o'clock

afterwards later

again once more *Try again!*

against **1** on the opposite side to *We played against your team and won.*
2 on or next to *He leant against the wall.*

age how old someone or something is

agent someone whose job is to arrange things for people *a travel agent*

agile able to move quickly and easily

agree to think the same as someone else

aground trapped on sand and rocks in shallow water. Ships sometimes run aground on rocks and are badly damaged.

ahead in front *I went on ahead to open the gate.*

aid **1** to help *We sent blankets to aid the victims of the earthquake.*
2 something that helps *a hearing aid*

aim **1** to point a gun at something *She aimed the gun at the target.* **2** to throw, kick, or shoot at something you are trying to hit *He aimed the ball into the far corner of the net.* **3** to try to do something *They aimed to finish in time for tea.*

air what everyone breathes

aircraft any aeroplane or helicopter *two aircraft*

air force a group of people trained to use aeroplanes for fighting

air-gun a gun that uses air instead of an explosive to make the bullets shoot out

air-hostess a woman whose job is to look after people travelling in an aeroplane

airport a place where people can get on or off aeroplanes

air-tight tightly closed so that air cannot get into it or out of it *an air-tight jar*

aisle (*say* ile *to rhyme with* tile) a path between groups of seats. Churches, cinemas, aeroplanes, and buses have aisles.

alarm **1** a sudden, frightened feeling *She cried out in alarm when she heard the strange noise.* **2** a warning sound or sign *a clock with an alarm*

album a book where you can keep things like stamps or photographs

alcohol a liquid that has no colour. One kind of alcohol is found in certain drinks such as beer and whisky.

alert lively and ready for anything

alight on fire

alive living

all **1** everyone or everything *Let's start singing. All together now . . .* **2** the whole of something.

alley a very narrow street

alligator a large animal that lives in rivers in America and China. It has short legs, a long body, and sharp teeth.

alligator

allotment a small piece of land that you can pay to use. People grow vegetables, fruit, and flowers on their allotments.

allow to let something happen *Are you allowed to watch that programme?*

all right **1** safe and well **2** I agree *All right, you can stay up.*

ally a person or country fighting on the same side

almond a kind of flat nut with a very hard shell

almost very nearly *We're almost home now.*

alone without others *She's working alone in the corner.*

along **1** from one end to the other *He ran along the top of the wall.* **2** *Come along!* Hurry up!

aloud in a voice that can be heard *Do not read to yourself – read aloud.*

alphabets

АБВГДЕЖЗИЙКЛМНОПР
СТУФХЦЧШЩЪЫЬЭЮЯ

ص ض ط ظ ع غ ف ق ك ل م ن ه و ي
ا ب ت ث ج ح خ د ذ ر ز س ش

ΑΒΓΔΕΖΗΘΙΚΛΜΝ
ΞΟΠΡΣΤΥΦΧΨΩ

म आ इ ई उ ऊ ऋ ॠ ऍ ऎ ए ऐ क ख ग घ ङ
च छ ज झ ञ ट ठ ड ढ ण त थ द ध न
प फ ब भ म य र ल व श ष स ह

alphabet   all the letters used in writing a language, arranged in order

already   **1** by this time *He was already there when we arrived*
2 before now *I've already done that.*

also   as well *jelly and also ice-cream*

altar   the table with a cross on it in a church

alter   to change

alteration   a change in someone or something *They had to make alterations to the uniform as it was too big for her.*

although   though

altogether   counting everything or everyone

aluminium   a very light metal, coloured like silver

always   at all times *He's always hungry.*

amateur   **1** someone who does something as a hobby
2 someone who takes part in a sport and is not paid

amaze   to surprise greatly *She amazed her friends by coming to school in an aeroplane.*

ambition   something that you want to do very much *Her ambition is to be a doctor.*

ambulance   a van for taking injured or ill people to hospital

ammunition   anything that is fired from a gun

among   in the middle of

amount   how much or how many there are *a large amount of money*

amuse   **1** to make someone laugh or smile
2 to make time pass pleasantly for someone *I was amusing myself with this puzzle.*

amusement   **1** an amused feeling *They watched in amusement as the baby took its first steps.*
2 something that entertains you

ancestor   a member of the same family who lived long ago

anchor   a heavy metal hook joined to a ship by a chain. It is dropped into the sea, where it digs into the bottom to keep the ship still.

anchor

ancient   very old *This church is ancient – it was built hundreds of years ago.*

angel   a messenger sent by God

anger   a strong feeling that you get when you are not pleased. It makes you want to fight or hurt someone. *She was filled with anger when she saw them teasing the cat.*

angle the corner where two lines meet

angler a fisherman who uses a rod, hook, and line

angry feeling anger

animal anything that lives and can move about. Birds, fish, snakes, wasps, and elephants are all animals

ankle the thin part of the leg where it is joined to the foot

anniversary a day when you remember something special that happened on the same day in another year *a wedding anniversary*

announce to say something in front of a lot of people *They announced the winner of the competition.*

annoy to make someone angry

annual 1 a book that comes out once a year
2 happening every year *an annual meeting*

anorak a waterproof jacket with a hood

another 1 a different one *Choose another hat – that one is too big.*
2 one more *No, you can't have another cake.*

answer 1 to say something to someone who has asked you a question *What is 6 × 7? Can anyone answer?*
2 something that is said or done in return *Do you think you will get an answer to your letter?*

ant a tiny insect

Antarctic the very cold sea and land in the south of the world

antelope a wild animal that looks like a deer. Antelope are found in Africa and parts of Asia.

antique (*say* an-teek) something old that is very valuable

anxious worried *She was anxious when he was late home.*

any 1 some *Have you any wool?*
2 at all *Are you any better?*

anybody, anyone any person

anything any thing *It's so dark, I can't see anything*

anywhere in any place

apart away from each other *London and Sydney are far apart.*

ape an animal like a large monkey with long arms and no tail. Chimpanzees and gorillas are apes.

apologize to say that you are sorry for doing something wrong

apparatus special things that you use for doing something *P.E. apparatus*

appeal to ask for something that you need *He appealed for help.*

appear 1 to come and be seen *He appeared from behind the curtain.*
2 to seem *It appears to be the wrong size.*

appearance 1 what someone looks like *His appearance was very untidy.*
2 coming so that you can be seen *The appearance of the rabbit surprised everyone.*

appendix the small tube inside the body that sometimes causes an illness called **appendicitis**

appetite the wish for food *She's been ill and has no appetite.*

antelope

applaud to clap to show that you are pleased

applause clapping

apple a round, crisp, juicy fruit

appoint to choose someone for a job *A new headmistress was appointed.*

appointment a time when you have arranged to go and see someone *an appointment at the dentist's*

approach to come near to

approximate nearly correct

apricot a round, soft, juicy fruit. It has a large stone in it and a thin, orange skin.

apron something worn over the front of the body to keep the clothes underneath clean

aqualung

aqualung a cylinder filled with air and joined to a tube. People strap aqualungs on their backs so that they can breathe under water.

aquarium a large, glass container where fish are kept

arch a curved part that helps to support a bridge or building

archery shooting at a target with a bow and arrow

architect (*say* arkitect) a person who draws plans for buildings

Arctic the very cold sea and land in the north of the world

area **1** an amount of surface *The area of a field is calculated by multiplying the length by the breadth.* **2** a part of a country or place *a no smoking area*

argue to talk about something with people who do not agree with you

argument talking in an angry or excited way to someone who does not agree with you

arithmetic finding out about numbers

arm the part of the body between the shoulder and the hand

armchair a comfortable chair with parts at the side for you to rest your arms on

armour **1** metal clothes worn in battles long ago **2** sheets of metal put round ships and tanks to protect them in war

armour 1

armpit the part underneath the top of the arm

arms weapons

army a large group of people trained to fight on land

around **1** all round *Around the castle there was a thick forest.*
2 here and there *Look around for it.*

arouse to wake someone up

arrange to put in order *Arrange the books in neat piles.*

arrangement something that it has been decided will happen *We made an arrangement to meet after school.*

arrest to take someone prisoner *The policeman arrested the thief.*

arrive to come to the end of a journey

arrow a pointed stick that is shot from a bow

art **1** drawing and painting
2 the ability to do something difficult

article a particular thing *A skirt is an article of clothing.*

artificial not natural because it has been made by people or machines *artificial flowers*

artist someone who draws or paints pictures

ascend (*say* a-send) to go up

ash **1** the grey powder left when something has been burned
2 a kind of tree

ashamed feeling very sorry and guilty about something

ashore on land *The sailors went ashore*

aside to one side *`Stand aside!*

ask to speak in order to find out or get something

asleep sleeping

aspirin a small white pill. You swallow it when you have a cold or a pain to make you feel better.

ass a donkey

assembly the time when the whole school meets together

assembly line a group of people working to put something together in a factory

assist to help

assistance help

assistant **1** someone whose job is to help someone more important *an assistant to the manager*
2 someone who serves in a shop

assorted with different sorts put together *a bag of assorted sweets*

asthma an illness that makes breathing difficult

astonish to surprise greatly

astonishment great surprise *They stared in astonishment at the spaceship.*

astronaut someone who travels in space

astronaut

astronomer someone who studies the sun, the stars, and the planets

astronomy finding out about the sun, the stars, and the planets

ate   see **eat**

athlete   someone who trains to be good at running, jumping, or throwing

atlas   a book of maps

atmosphere   the air around the earth

atom   one of the very tiny things that everything is made up of

attach   to join or fasten   *You must attach a label to your suitcase.*

attack   to start fighting in order to beat or hurt someone

attempt   to try   *He attempted to jump over the gate.*

attend   **1** to be in a place in order to take part in something   *She was asked to attend a meeting after school.* **2** to listen carefully   *You should attend to what the teacher says.*

attendance   being at a place in order to take part in something   *school attendance*

attention   **1** careful listening, reading, or thinking **2** *pay attention* take notice

attic   a room or rooms inside the roof of a house

attract   **1** to interest   *The toy attracted the baby's attention and he stopped crying.* **2** to make something come nearer *The magnet attracted the small piece of metal.*

attractive   very pleasant to look at

auction   (*say* oction) a sale when things are sold to the people who offer the most money for them

audience   people who have come to a place to see or hear something

aunt   your uncle's wife or the sister of one of your parents

author   someone who writes books or stories

authority   the power to make other people do as you say   *The police have the authority to stop speeding cars.*

autograph   your name written by yourself

automatic   able to work on its own and control itself. Slot machines are automatic.

autumn   the part of the year when leaves fall off the trees and it gets colder

available   ready for you to use   *In winter sledges are available in the shops.*

avalanche   a large amount of snow, rock, or ice sliding suddenly down a mountain

avenue   a road, often with trees along each side

average   ordinary or usual   *average marks   average height for his age*

avoid   to keep out of the way of someone or something

await   to wait for

awake   not sleeping

award   a prize that you have worked for   *There is an award for the neatest writing.*

aware   knowing about something   *She was aware that if she were late home her mother would worry.*

away   **1** not here   *She was away yesterday.* **2** to another place   *He ran away.*

awful   very bad

awkward   **1** clumsy **2** difficult to deal with   *an awkward customer* **3** not convenient   *an awkward time*

axe a tool for chopping

axle a rod that goes through the centre of wheels to join them to something *the car axle*

B b ——————————

baby a very young child

bachelor a man who has not married

back 1 the side opposite the front
2 the part of the body between the neck and the bottom or tail

backward, backwards
1 towards the back
2 in the opposite way to usual

bacon dried or salty meat from a pig's back or sides

badge something worn pinned or stitched to clothes. It shows which group someone belongs to or how important he is. *a school badge, a sheriff's badge*

badger a grey animal that digs holes in the ground. It has a white face with black stripes on it.

baggage luggage, suitcases

bail 1 one of the two pieces of wood put on top of the stumps in cricket
2 to throw water out of a boat, using buckets *Bail out the water before we sink.*

bait food put on a hook or in a trap to catch animals

bake to cook inside an oven

baker someone whose job is to make or sell bread and cakes

balance 1 a pair of scales for weighing things
2 to keep or make something steady *The seal is balancing a ball on the end of its nose.*

balcony 1 a platform with a rail round it outside an upstairs window
2 the seats upstairs in a cinema or theatre

bald without any hair on the head

bale 1 a large bundle or package *a bale of hay*
2 *to bale out* to jump out of an aeroplane with a parachute

ball 1 a round object used in games
2 a big party with a lot of dancing

ballerina a woman who is a ballet dancer

ballet a story told on the stage in dancing, mime, and music

balloon 1 a small, coloured, rubber bag that you can blow up and burst
2 a bag filled with hot air or gas so that it floats in the sky

balloon 2

bamboo a tall plant with stiff, hollow stems. It grows in very hot countries and is used for making furniture.

ban   to say that someone must never do a certain thing   *They have banned roller-skating in the playground.*

banana   a long fruit with a thick yellow skin

band   **1** a group of people   *a band of robbers*
2 some people playing musical instruments together
3 a strip of material. Bands are put round things to decorate them or to keep them together.   *a rubber band*

bandage   a strip of material for wrapping round part of the body that has been hurt

bandit   an outlaw who is a robber

bang   **1** the sudden, loud, hard sound an explosion makes
2 to hit or shut with a loud noise   *Don't bang the door!*

bangle   a ring worn round the arm

banish   to send someone away from a place as a punishment   *The wicked king banished the princess from the land for seven years.*

banisters   the posts and rail at the side of a staircase

banjo   a musical instrument with strings that you play with your fingers. It is smaller and rounder than a guitar.

bank   **1** a place that looks after money and valuable things for people
2 the ground near the edge of a river, canal, or lake

banner   a kind of flag

banquet   a big feast given by someone important

bar   **1** a long piece of wood or metal
2 a block of chocolate, toffee, or soap
3 a place that serves food and drinks at a counter   *a coffee bar*

barbed wire   wire with sharp spikes in it, used for making fences

barber   a man whose job is to cut men's and boys' hair

bare   without any clothes or covering

bargain   **1** a promise to give something in return for something else   *They made a bargain to swap the toys.*
2 something that costs much less than usual   *You can get bargains at jumble sales.*

barge   a long boat with a flat bottom. Barges are used on canals and rivers.

barges

bark   **1** to make the hard, loud sound a dog makes
2 the hard covering round a tree's trunk and branches

barley   a plant grown by farmers. Its seed is used for making food and beer.

barn   a large building on a farm, where things are stored

barn

barracks an army building where soldiers live together

barrel 1 a round, wooden container with flat ends *a barrel of beer*
2 the part like a tube at the front of a gun

barren without plants *barren land*

barrier a fence or something that stands in the way

barrow a small cart that is pushed

base the bottom part of something *The base of the statue was made of wood.*

basement the rooms in a building that are below the ground

bash to hit very hard

bashful shy

basic most important *basic information*

basin a bowl

basket a bag made of straw or cane

bat 1 an animal like a mouse with wings
2 a piece of wood for hitting a ball in a game
3 to have a turn at playing with a bat in a game like cricket

batch a number of things together *a batch of letters*

bath 1 a large container filled with water. You sit in it and wash yourself all over.
2 to put a baby or animal in water and wash it *Bath the muddy puppy.*

bathe 1 to play or swim in the sea or a river *They bathed in the pool.*
2 to wash part of yourself carefully and gently *He bathed his cut finger.*

bathroom the room where you can have a bath or wash

batsman the person who uses the bat in cricket or rounders

batter 1 a liquid made from flour, egg, and milk. It is used for making pancakes and frying fish.
2 to damage something by hitting it often *The wind battered down the fence.*

battery a closed container with electricity inside it. You put batteries inside things like torches and radios to make them work.

batteries

battle fighting between groups of people

bawl to shout or cry loudly *The hungry baby was bawling.*

bay a place where the coast bends inwards and sea fills the space

bayonet a sharp blade that can be fixed to a gun

bazaar a group of stalls selling different things to get money for something *a church bazaar*

BBC short for **British Broadcasting Corporation**

beach land by the edge of the sea. It is usually covered with sand or small stones.

bead a small, round object with a hole through the middle. Beads are threaded on string to make necklaces and bracelets.

beak   the hard part round a bird's mouth

beaker   a kind of tall cup. Some beakers have no handle.

beam   **1** a long piece of wood
2 a line of light   *the torch beam*
3 to smile very happily

beans

bean   a vegetable. Beans are round seeds and some sorts grow inside long green pods that can also be eaten. *French beans, broad beans*

beanbag   a small cloth bag filled with dried beans, used in games

bear 4

bear   **1** to carry *The donkey bore the load patiently*
2 to put up with   *He could not have borne any more pain*
3 to give birth to   *Their baby was born yesterday.*
4 a large animal with very thick fur

beard   hair growing on a man's chin

beast   **1** any big animal
2 a horrible person

beat   **1** to do better than someone else *You beat me last time.*
2 to hit often   *The horse had been beaten with a stick.*
3 to stir very hard

beautiful   **1** very attractive
a beautiful face
2 very pleasant   *a beautiful day*

beauty   something or someone beautiful

became   see **become**

because   for the reason that   *I got wet because it rained.*

beckon   to move your hand to show someone that you want them to come nearer

become   to come to be   *It suddenly became very dark.*

bedroom   the room where you sleep

bee   an insect that can fly, sting, and make honey

beech   a kind of tree

beef   meat from a cow, bull, or ox

beehive   a kind of box for keeping bees in

beer   a strong brown drink

beetle   an insect with hard wing cases

beetles

beetroot a round, dark red vegetable

before 1 earlier than *I was here before you.*
2 in front of *It vanished before my eyes.*

began see **begin**

beggar someone who lives by asking other people for money, clothes, or food

begin to start *I'm beginning to understand. He began school last week. I have begun to learn the piano.*

beginner someone who has just started learning something

beginning the start of something

begun see **begin**

behave 1 to show good or bad manners in front of other people *He's behaved badly, she's behaving well*
2 *Behave yourself!* Be good!

behaviour how you behave

behind at the back of *He hid behind the wall.*

belief what someone believes

believe to feel sure that something is true

bell a hollow piece of metal that rings when it is hit

bells

bellow to shout and make a lot of noise like an angry bull

belly the stomach

belong 1 to be someone's *That pen belongs to me.*
2 to be part of something *to belong to the Scouts*
3 to be in the proper place *Your coat belongs on the peg, not on the floor.*

below underneath *Write your address below your name.*

belt a stiff band worn round the waist

bench a wooden or stone seat for more than one person

bend 1 to make something curved or not straight
2 to lean over so that your head is nearer to the ground *He bent down and looked at his shoes.*

beneath underneath

bent see **bend**

berry any small, round fruit with seeds in it. Some berries are poisonous.

beside at the side of *a house beside the sea*

besides as well as *Ten people besides me also won prizes.*

best better than any other *my best friend*

betray 1 to give away a secret
2 to give information about your friends or country to the enemy *A spy betrays his country's secrets.*

better 1 more able *better than me at swimming*
2 well again *I'm better now, thank you.*

between 1 in the middle of two people or things *I sat between Mum and Dad.*
2 among *Share the money between you.*

beware be careful *Beware of the dog.*

bewildered   very puzzled

bewitched   under a spell

beyond   further than   *Don't go beyond the end of the road.*

Bible   the holy book that is read in all Christian churches

bicycle, bike   a machine with two wheels and pedals, that you can ride.

bill   **1** a piece of paper that tells you how much money you owe   *He paid all his bills.*
2 a bird's beak

billiards   a game played on a long table with rods used to hit three small balls

billy-goat   a male goat

bind   to tie together   *The prisoner's hands were bound behind his back.*

bingo   a game where each person has a card with different numbers on it. Each player marks the numbers off when they are called.

binoculars   a special pair of glasses like two tubes joined together. When you look through them, things far away seem much nearer.

binoculars

bird   any animal with feathers, wings, and a beak

birth   the beginning of life, when a baby leaves its mother and starts to breathe

birthday   the day each year when you remember the day someone was born

biscuit   a kind of small, thin, dry cake

bishop   a priest who is in charge of other priests

bit   **1** a very small amount of something
2 the part of a bridle that goes into a horse's mouth
3 see **bite**

bitch   a female dog

bite   to use the teeth to cut into something   *Your dog's bitten me. Stop biting your nails!   She bit into the apple.*

bitter   not sweet

blackberry   a small, soft, black berry that grows on bushes

blackbird   a bird often seen in gardens. The male is black with an orange beak, but the female is brown.

blackbirds

blackboard   a piece of black or dark green wood that you can write on with chalk

blacksmith   someone whose job is to make horseshoes and other things out of iron

blade   **1** the flat, sharp part of a knife or sword
2 something shaped like a blade   *a blade of grass*

blame   to say that it is because of a certain person or thing that something bad has happened   *He blamed his broken pen for his untidy writing.*

blancmange   (*say* bla-monj) a kind of jelly made from sugar, milk, and flour

blank   with nothing written or drawn on it   *a blank page*

blanket   a thick cover used on a bed

blast   **1** sudden, rushing wind or air   *A blast of cold air came through the open door.*
2 to blow up   *The miners used explosives to blast away the rocks.*

blaze   to burn brightly   *The fire was blazing in the grate.*

blazer   a kind of jacket. A blazer usually has a badge on its top pocket.

bleach   to make something white

bleak   cold, miserable, and windy   *a bleak day*

bleat   to make the sound sheep make

bleed   to lose blood   *His nose bled for ten minutes.*

blend   to mix together

bless   to ask God to look after someone and make them happy   *God bless you.*

blew   see **blow**

blind   **1** not able to see
2 a screen that you pull down to cover a window

blink   to close your eyes and open them again very quickly

blister   a small swelling on the skin. It has liquid inside and hurts when you touch it.

blizzard   a storm with a lot of snow and wind

block   **1** a thick piece of something solid like wood or stone
2 to be in the way so that something cannot get through

blond, blonde   with fair hair

blood   a red liquid that moves round inside the body

bloom   to be in flower   *Roses bloom in summer.*

blossom   flowers on a tree

blot   a spot of ink spilt on something

blotting-paper   thick paper that dries ink quickly

blouse   a piece of clothing worn on the top half of the body by women and girls

blow   **1** to make air come out of the mouth   *She blew out the candles and cut the cake.*
2 to move along with the wind   *Tiles were blown off the roof.*

bluebell   a wild plant with flowers like tiny blue bells

blunder   **1** to make a big mistake
2 to move about very clumsily

blunt   not sharp   *a blunt knife*

blur   to make something look not clear. Smudged writing is blurred.

blush   to go red in the face because you feel shy or guilty

boar   a wild pig

board   **1** a long piece of thin wood
2 stiff cardboard
3 to get on an aeroplane, bus, ship, or train

boar

17

boast　to talk in a way that shows you are much too proud of yourself and what you can do　*He boasted about his football skills.*

boat　something that floats and has room in it for taking people or things over water

boats

body　**1** all of a person or animal that can be seen or touched　*a dead body*　**2** all of a person except his legs, arms, and head

bodyguard　a person or persons whose job is to protect someone

boomerang

bog　a piece of ground so wet and soft that your feet sink into it

boil　**1** to heat liquid until it bubbles　**2** to cook something in hot, bubbling water　**3** a big painful spot on the skin

boiler　a large container in which water is heated

bold　brave and not afraid

bolt　**1** to rush off　*The frightened horse bolted.*　**2** to swallow food quickly without chewing it　**3** a kind of sliding fastener used on doors　*He fastened the bolt on the back door.*　**4** a thick metal pin like a screw　*a nut and bolt*

bomb　a weapon that blows up and does a lot of damage

bone　any of the separate parts of a skeleton

bonfire　a large fire built in the open air

bonnet　**1** a hat that is tied under the chin　**2** the part of a car that covers the engine

book　**1** sheets of paper fastened together and fixed to a cover　**2** to arrange for a seat to be kept for you. You can book seats on coaches and trains and at theatres and cinemas.

bookcase　a piece of furniture made for holding books

boom　to make a loud, deep sound　*The guns boomed away in the distance.*

boomerang　a curved stick that comes back to the person who throws it

boot　**1** a kind of shoe that also covers the ankle　**2** the part of a car for carrying luggage

border **1** the narrow part along the edge of something *a border of flowers*
2 the line where two countries meet *She needed her passport to cross the border.*

bore **1** to make someone tired by being dull *a boring film*
2 to make a hole with a tool
3 see **bear**

born, borne see **bear**

borrow to get the use of something for a short time and agree to give it back

boss the person who is in charge

both the two of them *He took both of the cakes.*

bother **1** to worry or annoy someone *Is the loud music bothering you?*
2 to take trouble over doing something *He never bothers to tidy his room.*

bottle a glass container for liquids that is narrow at the top *a milk bottle*

bottom **1** the lowest part of anything
2 the part of the body that you sit on

bough (*rhymes with* cow) a large branch

bracelets

bought see **buy**

boulder a large, smooth rock

bounce to spring back after hitting something hard

bound **1** to leap
2 see **bind**

boundary a line marking the edge of some land

bouquet (*say* boo-kay) a bunch of flowers

bow[1] (*rhymes with* go)
1 a strip of bent wood with string joining each end. It is used for shooting arrows.
2 a wooden rod with strong hairs stretched along it and joining each end, for playing the violin
3 a knot with loops *a bow in her hair*

bow[2] (*rhymes with* cow) to bend forwards to show respect *He bowed to the Queen.*

bowl **1** a round, open container for liquid or food
2 to throw a ball to the batsman

box **1** a container with a lid *a cardboard box*
2 to fight with the fists

boy a male child or teenager

brace a piece of wire worn across teeth to straighten them

bracelet beads, a chain, or a ring worn round the arm

braces a pair of straps worn to keep up trousers

bracket **1** a piece of metal fixed to a wall to support something *The shelf rests on two brackets.*
2 one of a pair of marks like these ( )

brag to talk in a way that shows you are much too proud of yourself and what you can do *She bragged that she was the best runner in the class.*

brain   the part inside the top of the head that controls the body. It also makes people able to think and remember.

brake   the part of a car or bicycle that makes it slow down or stop

bramble   a blackberry bush or a prickly bush like it

branch   a part that sticks out from the trunk of a tree

brand   **1** a mark to show the maker or owner   *The farmer put a brand of blue dye on the sheep's back.*
2 a certain kind of goods   *a new brand of tea*

brass   a yellow metal made by mixing copper with zinc

brave   **1** ready and able to bear pain or danger
2 a male American Indian

bravery   the ability to be brave

bray   to make the harsh sound a donkey makes

bread   a food made by baking dough in loaves

breadth   the measurement or distance across something

break   **1** to snap, smash, or crack   *The cup broke when I dropped it.*
2 to fail to keep a law or promise   *He's broken the rules.*
3 a short rest from work   *take a break*

breakfast   the first meal of the day

breath   the air that a person breathes

breathe   to take air into your lungs through your nose or mouth and send it out again   *She was breathing quickly after the race.*

breed   to keep animals in order to get young ones from them   *Last year he bred rabbits.*

breeze   a gentle wind

brick   a small, oblong block used in building

bride   a woman on the day she gets married

bridegroom   a man on the day he gets married

bridesmaid   a girl or woman who walks behind the bride at her wedding

bridge   something built to go over a river, railway, or road

bridges

bridle   the parts of a harness used for controlling a horse

brief   short   *a brief talk*

brigade   an organized group of people in uniform   *the fire brigade*

bright   **1** shining   *a bright star*
2 intelligent   *a bright boy*
3 cheerful   *a bright smile*

brilliant   very bright   *brilliant light*
a brilliant scientist

brim   **1** the edge round the top of a container   *a cup filled to the brim*   **2** the part of a hat that sticks out round the edge

bring   **1** to carry here   *Bring your book.*   **2** to lead here   *Yesterday he brought his friend.*

brink   the edge of a dangerous place   *He trembled on the brink of the precipice.*

brisk   quick and lively

bristle   a short, stiff hair like the hairs on a brush

brittle   likely to break or snap

broad   measuring a lot from side to side   *a broad river*

broadcast   a television or radio programme

broke, broken   see **break**

bronze   a brown metal made by mixing copper and tin

brooch   (*rhymes with* coach)   a piece of jewellery worn pinned to clothing

brook   a small stream

broom   a sweeping brush with a long handle

broth   a thin soup made from meat and vegetables

brother   a man or boy who has the same parents as another person

brought   see **bring**

brow   **1** the forehead   *He wiped the sweat from his brow.*   **2** the top of a hill   *When they reached the brow of the hill they rested.*

Brownie   a junior Guide

bruise   a coloured mark that comes on the skin when it has been hit hard

brush   a tool with short, stiff hairs. Brushes are used for making hair tidy, cleaning, sweeping, scrubbing, and painting.

bubble   **1** a small ball of air inside liquid   **2** to be full of bubbles

buck   **1** a male deer, hare, or rabbit   **2** to leap like a horse about to throw someone off its back

bucket   a container with a handle but no lid, used for carrying liquid

buckle   a kind of fastening used on belts or straps

bud   a flower or leaf before it has opened

Buddhism   the religion following the teachings of Buddha

budge   to move slightly

budgerigar   a small, brightly coloured bird kept as a pet

buffalo   a kind of wild ox. Buffaloes are found in Africa, India, and North America.

buffet   (*say* buffay)   a place where you can get drinks and snacks

bugle   a small, brass musical instrument that you blow into

build   to make something by putting things carefully on top of one another   *Last autumn we built a huge bonfire.*

building   something that has been built. Houses, schools, theatres, shops, and churches are all buildings

built   see **build**

bulb   **1** the part of a lamp that gives light   **2** something that looks like an onion and is planted in soil. Daffodils, tulips, and some other flowers grow from bulbs.

bulge   to swell out   *His pockets were bulging with conkers.*

bulk   a large amount

bull a male ox, elephant, or whale

bulldozer a heavy machine for clearing land

bulldozer

bullet a small lump of metal made to be fired from a gun

bullock a young, male ox

bully someone who attacks or threatens a weaker person

bulrush a tall plant that grows near water

bump **1** to knock against something by accident *The giant bumped his head on the ceiling.*
2 a swelling *a painful bump on the head*

bumper a bar along the front or back of a car. It protects the car if it hits something.

bunch a group of things joined or tied together

bundle a group of things tied together *a bundle of sticks*

bungalow a house without any upstairs rooms

bunk a bed that has another bed above or below it

buoy (*say* boy)
a thing in the sea to warn ships about danger

burden something that has to be carried

burglar someone who gets into a building to steal things

burial (*say* berrial)
the burying of a dead person

burn **1** to hurt or damage something with fire or heat
2 to be on fire

burrow a hole in the ground that an animal lives in *Rabbits live in burrows.*

burst to break open suddenly because there is too much inside

bury to put something or someone in a hole in the ground and cover it over

bush a plant that looks like a small tree

business (*say* biznis)
1 a person's work *My father's business is selling cars.*
2 a shop or firm or industry

bustle to hurry in a busy or fussy way

busy **1** doing things all the time
2 full of activity *a busy street*

butcher someone whose job is to cut up meat and sell it

butter a yellow food made from cream. It is spread on bread.

buttercup a wild flower with shiny yellow petals

butterfly an insect with large white or coloured wings

butterflies

butterscotch hard toffee made from sugar and butter

button a fastener sewn on clothes. It fits into a hole or loop.

buy to get something by giving money for it *I bought this bike from him yesterday.*

buzz to make the sound a bee makes

C c

cab 1 the part of a lorry, bus, or train where the driver sits
2 a taxi

cabbage a vegetable with a lot of green leaves

cabin 1 a room in a ship or aeroplane
2 a small hut *a log cabin*

cabinet a kind of cupboard with drawers

cable strong, thick wire or rope

cackle to laugh and make the sound a hen makes

cactus a plant with a thick green stem and thick green branches, covered in prickles. Cacti grow in hot, dry places and do not need much water

café (*say* kaffay)
a place where you can buy a drink, a snack, or a meal

cafeteria a kind of café where you fetch your own food from the counter

cage a large box with bars across it for keeping animals in

cake a food made with flour, butter, eggs, and sugar

calamity something very bad that happens suddenly

calculator a machine that can do sums

calendar a list showing all the days, weeks, and months in a year

calf 1 a young cow, elephant, or whale *two calves*
2 the back part of the leg between the knee and the ankle

caliper a pair of metal bars worn to support a weak leg

call 1 to speak loudly
2 to give a name to someone or something
3 to tell someone to come to you *The mother called the children.*

calm (*say* karm)
1 still *a calm sea*
2 not noisy or excited

calves more than one **calf**

came see **come**

camel a big animal with one or two humps on its back. Camels are used instead of horses in deserts, because they can travel for a long time without eating or drinking.

camels

camera a machine for taking photographs

camouflage
to hide something by making it look like other things that are near it. Most wild animals are camouflaged by their colour or shape, when they are not moving.

camp **1** a group of tents or huts where people live for a short time
2 *to go camping* to have a holiday living in a tent

can **1** to be able to *I can swim – he can't. He could read before he started school. I couldn't.*
2 a tin *a can of coke*

canal a kind of river made by people, so that boats can go straight from one place to another

canary a small yellow bird that sings

cancer a serious disease in which lumps grow in the body

capsule 2

candle a stick of wax with string through the centre. It gives light as it burns.

candlestick something to hold a candle

cane **1** the hard stem of some plants
2 a long, thin stick

cannon a big gun that fires heavy metal balls

canoe (*say* ca-<u>noo</u>)
a light, narrow boat that you move by using a paddle

canteen a kind of café that sells food to people in a school, factory, or office

canter one of the ways a horse can move. It is faster than a trot but slower than a gallop.

canvas strong material for making things like tents

capable able to do something *You're capable of better work.*

capacity the largest amount a container can hold *The capacity of a milk bottle is one pint.*

cape a short cloak

capital **1** the most important city in a country *London is the capital of England.*
2 one of the big letters put at the beginning of names and sentences. A, B, C, D, and so on are **capital letters**

capsule **1** something that looks like a sweet, but has medicine inside. It has to be swallowed whole.
2 a separate part at the front of a spaceship. It can move on its own away from the main part.

captain **1** an officer in the army or navy
2 someone who is in charge of a team

captive a person or animal that has been captured

capture **1** to take prisoner
2 to get something by fighting for it

caramel soft toffee

caravan a house on wheels that can be pulled by a car or truck from place to place

caravan

carriage 2

carburettor the part of an engine that mixes the petrol with air

card **1** thick, stiff paper
2 a piece of card with a picture and a message on it. You send cards to people at special times like Christmas.
3 one of a set of small pieces of card with numbers or pictures on them, used in games

cardboard very thick, strong paper

cardigan a kind of knitted jacket

care **1** worry or trouble
2 *to take care of* to look after
3 *to care for* to look after
4 *to care about* to be very interested in something

careful making sure that you do things safely and well *a careful driver*

careless not careful

caretaker someone whose job is to look after a building

cargo things taken by ship or aeroplane from one place to another *cargoes of fruit*

carnation a garden plant with white, pink, or red flowers that smell very sweet

carnival a colourful procession with people wearing fancy dress

carol a happy song sung at Christmas

carpenter someone whose job is to make things out of wood

carpet a thick cover for the floor

carriage **1** one of the separate parts of a train where passengers sit
2 a vehicle on wheels pulled by horses

carrot an orange vegetable shaped like a cone

carry to take people, animals, or things from one place to another *We carried the shopping bags all the way home.*

cart a kind of box on wheels. It is pulled by a horse or pushed by a person

carton a light container made of cardboard or plastic

cartoon **1** a film that uses drawings instead of actors *a Mickey Mouse cartoon*
2 a drawing that tells a joke

cartridge a case or tube holding film, tape or ink

carve **1** to cut wood or stone to make a picture or a shape
2 to cut off slices of meat

cascade a waterfall

case **1** a container *a pencil case*
2 a suitcase

cash coins or paper money

cassette a small, closed container with a reel of tape inside it for recording or playing sounds

cast **1** a shape made by pouring liquid metal or plaster into a mould
2 all the actors in a play
3 to throw *He cast his net into the sea to catch fish.*

castaway someone who has been shipwrecked

castle a large, strong house with very thick, stone walls. Castles were built long ago to keep the people inside them safe from their enemies.

catalogue a complete list

catapult a piece of elastic joined to a stick shaped like a Y for shooting small stones

catch **1** to capture
2 to get hold of something
3 to get an illness *I caught a cold last week.*

caterpillar a long, creeping creature that will turn into a butterfly or moth

caterpillars

cathedral a big, important church *Durham Cathedral*

catkin one of the tiny flowers that hang down in clusters on some trees

cattle cows and bulls kept by a farmer

caught see **catch**

cauldron a large pot used for cooking *a witch's cauldron*

cauliflower a vegetable with a thick white stalk covered in small, hard, white flowers

cause to make something happen *The wind caused the door to slam.*

cautious only doing what is safe *a cautious man*

cavalry a group of men trained to fight while riding horses

cave a big hole under the ground or inside a mountain

cavern a large cave

cease to stop doing something

ceiling the surface above you in a room *Stand on a ladder to paint the ceiling.*

celebrate to do special things to show you are very happy about something. Every year people celebrate Easter.

celebration a party for something special

celery a vegetable with white stalks that can be eaten raw

cell **1** one of the small rooms where prisoners are kept in a prison
2 the tiniest part of a living thing

cellar a room underneath a building. Cellars are used for storing things.

Celsius a way of measuring temperature that gives 0 degrees for freezing water and 100 degrees for boiling water

cement a mixture of clay and lime used in building to stick things together

cemetery a place where dead people are buried

centigrade an older name for Celsius

centimetre a measure for length *a ruler is 30 centimetres long.*

centipede a long, creeping creature with a lot of tiny legs

centipede

centre the middle of something

century a hundred years

cereal **1** any plant grown by farmers for its seed
2 a food made from the seed of cereal plants and eaten at breakfast with milk *Weetabix is my favourite cereal*

ceremony (*say* serimony)
something important and serious that is
done in front of other people
a marriage ceremony

certain **1** sure *Are you certain?*
2 one in particular *a certain person*

certificate a piece of paper that says
you have done something special

chaffinch a small bird. Its front is red
and it has white marks on its wings.

chaffinch

chain a line made of metal rings
fastened together

chair a seat for one person

chalet (*say* shallay)
a small, wooden house with a large roof

chalk **1** a kind of soft white rock
2 a soft white stick used for writing on
blackboards

challenge to ask someone to try to do
better than you at something

champion **1** someone who is the best
in their sport
2 an animal or plant that wins a
competition

championship a competition to
decide on the champion

chance **1** a time when you can do
something that you cannot do at other
times *This is your last chance.*
2 the way things happen that have not
been planned *I saw him by chance on
the bus.*

change **1** to make or become different
Tadpoles change into frogs.
2 to give something and get something
in return *They changed places with
each other.*
3 the money that you get back when
you give more money than is needed to
pay for something *The shop-
assistant gave him the change.*

channel **1** a narrow sea *the English
Channel*
2 a groove in the ground that water
moves along
3 the name given to a television
station *Which channel shall we
watch?*

chapel a kind of church

chapter a part of a book

character **1** someone in a story
2 the sort of person you are

charge **1** to ask a certain price
They charge 70p for a school dinner.
2 to rush at something to attack it
3 *in charge* with the job of telling other
people what they should do or how
they should do it

chariot

chariot a kind of cart with two wheels,
pulled by horses. Chariots were used
long ago for fighting and racing.

charity any group of people who raise money to help others *Which charities does your school support?*

charm **1** a magic spell
2 a small ornament worn to bring good luck
3 to cast a spell over someone or something

chart **1** a big map
2 a large sheet of paper with information on it

chase to run after and try to catch a person or animal

chat to talk in a friendly way about things that are not important

chatter **1** to talk a lot or very quickly
2 to make a rattling noise *His teeth chattered with fear.*

chauffeur (*say* show-fur)
someone whose job is to drive another person's car for them

cheap costing less than usual

cheat **1** to make another person believe what is not true so that you can get something from them
2 to try to do well in a test or game, by breaking the rules

check **1** to go over something to make sure it is correct
2 a pattern of squares

check-out the place in a shop where you pay for what you have bought

cheek **1** the side of the face below the eye
2 rude behaviour or speech

cheer to shout to show you are pleased or that you want your team to win

cheerful looking or sounding happy *a cheerful face*

cheese food made by stirring milk until it becomes solid

chemist someone whose job is to make or sell medicines

cherry a small, round, red or black fruit with a stone in it

cheque (*say* check)
a special form that a person can sign and use instead of money to pay for something

chest **1** a big, strong box
2 the front part of the body between the neck and the waist

chestnut **1** a kind of tree
2 the shiny brown nut that grows on a chestnut tree

chew **1** to keep biting food while you eat it
2 a kind of sweet

chicken a young bird kept for its meat and eggs

chicken-pox an illness that gives you red spots that itch

chief **1** the most important
2 the person in charge

child **1** a young boy or girl
2 a son or daughter *two children*

chill **1** a bad cold that makes you feel hot and dizzy
2 to make something cold

chime to make a tune like church bells

chimney a tall pipe inside the wall of a house to take away the smoke from a fire

chimpanzee an African animal like a large monkey with long arms and no tail

chimpanzee

chin the part of the face that is under the mouth

china cups, saucers, and plates made of very thin, delicate pottery

chip 1 a small piece of potato that is fried
2 to break or knock small pieces off something *a chipped vase*
3 a small electronic part in a computer

chisel a tool with a short, sharp edge, for cutting stone or wood

chocolate sweet food made from cocoa and sugar

choice 1 choosing *a choice of three different flavours of ice-cream*
2 what you have chosen

choir (*say* kwire)
a group of people who sing together

choke 1 to find it hard to get your breath because of something in your throat *The smoke made him choke.*
2 to block up something *The pond was choked with weeds.*

choose to take one thing instead of another, because you want to *Which car have you chosen? Last time you chose to go to the zoo.*

chop 1 to cut something by hitting it hard with a sharp tool
2 a small, thick slice of pork or lamb

chopsticks a pair of thin sticks held in one hand that Chinese and Japanese people use instead of a knife and fork

chorus (*say* ko-russ)
the words repeated after every verse in a poem or song

chose, chosen see **choose**

christen to give a baby its name in church and welcome it into God's family *The minister christened the baby yesterday.*

Christian someone who believes in Jesus Christ

Christmas the 25th December when Jesus Christ's birthday is celebrated

chrome, chromium (*say* krome, krome-ium)
a bright, shiny metal that looks like silver

chrysalis (*say* kriss-a-liss)
the cover a caterpillar makes round itself before it changes into a butterfly or moth

chrysanthemum an autumn flower with a lot of petals that grows in gardens

chuckle to laugh to yourself

chunk a thick lump *a chunk of cheese*

church a building where people worship God

churn 1 a large container for milk
2 a machine for turning milk into butter

chopsticks

cigar tobacco leaves that are rolled and then smoked

cigarette a thin tube of paper with tobacco inside it for smoking

cinders the grey pieces left when coal has finished burning

cinema a place where people go to see films

circle **1** the shape of a coin or wheel. The edge of a circle is always the same distance from the centre
2 the curved line round the edge of a circle

circular like a circle

circus a show held in a big tent or building with animals, acrobats, and clowns

city a big town

claim to ask for something that belongs to you *She claimed her lost property.*

clang to make the loud, ringing sound a heavy metal door makes when you shut it

clank to make the hard sound that heavy metal chains make when they bang against each other

clap to make a noise by hitting the palm of one hand with the palm of the other

clash **1** to make the sound cymbals make
2 to disagree with someone

clasp to hold tightly

class a group of pupils who learn things together

clatter to make the rattling sound a horse's hooves make on the road

claw one of the hard, sharp nails that some animals have on their feet

clay a sticky kind of earth used for making things, because it keeps its shape and goes hard

clean **1** not dirty *a clean face*
2 to make something clean *Clean your teeth.*

clear **1** easy to understand, see, or hear *a clear photograph, a clear voice*
2 free from things you do not want *a clear road, a clear day*
3 to make something clear *Please clear the table.*

clench to close your teeth, fingers, or fist tightly to show that you are determined to do something

clerk (*rhymes with* park) someone who sorts out papers and writes letters in an office

clever able to learn and understand things easily

click the short, sharp sound an electric light switch makes

cliff a steep rock close to the sea

climate the sort of weather that a place usually gets at different times of the year

climb to go up or down something high

cling to hold tightly on to someone or something *The child was afraid and clung to its mother.*

clinic **1** a kind of hospital
2 a kind of surgery where doctors work together

clip **1** to cut something with scissors or a tool like scissors *He clipped the hedge.*
2 a fastener for keeping things together or in place *a paper clip*

cloak a very loose coat without sleeves

cloakroom the room where you hang your coat

clock a machine that shows you what time it is

clocks

clockwise   in the direction a clock's hands move in

clockwork   able to work when it is wound up like a clock. Clockwork toys can move by themselves.

close[1]   (*rhymes with* dose)
1 very near   *close to the fire*
2 careful   *a close look*
3 a street closed at one end

close[2]   (*rhymes with* doze)
1 to shut   *All the shops are closing early today*
2 to end   *The village shop is closing down.*

cloth   **1** material for making things like clothes and curtains
2 a piece of cloth for cleaning or covering something

clothes, clothing   things worn to cover the body

cloud   **1** something white, grey, or black that floats in the sky. Clouds are made of drops of water that often fall as rain.
2 dust or smoke that looks like a cloud

clout   to hit hard with your hand

clover   a wild flower. Each of its leaves is like three small leaves joined together.

clown   someone in a circus who wears funny clothes and make-up and makes people laugh

club   **1** a group of people who meet together because they are interested in the same thing
2 a thick stick used as a weapon
3 a black clover leaf printed on some playing-cards
the ace of clubs

cluck   to make a noise like a hen

clue   something that helps you to find the answer to a puzzle

clump   a group of trees or plants growing close together

clumsy   likely to knock things over or drop things, because you move badly

clung   see **cling**

cluster   **1** a group of things growing together   *a cluster of berries*
2 a group of people, animals, or things gathered round something
The horses clustered round the water-hole.

clutch   **1** to snatch at something
2 to hold tightly
3 part of a car's mechanical system

coach   **1** a bus that takes people on long journeys
2 one of the separate parts of a train, where passengers sit
3 someone who trains people in a sport

coach 1

coal   hard, black rock that is burned to make heat

coarse   not delicate or smooth. Sacks are made of coarse material.

coast   the edge of land next to the sea

coat   something with long sleeves that people put on top of other clothes when they go out

cobbler   someone whose job is to mend shoes

cobweb   a thin, sticky net spun by a spider to trap insects

cockerel   a young, male bird kept with hens

cocoa   a brown powder used to make a hot drink that tastes of chocolate

coconut a big, round, hard seed that grows on palm trees. It has a sweet white food and liquid inside.

cod a large sea fish that can be eaten

code **1** a set of signs or letters for sending messages secretly or quickly
2 a set of rules *the Highway code*

coffee a hot drink. It is made from roasted beans crushed into a brown powder.

coffin the long box in which a dead person is put

coil to wind rope or wire into rings

coin a piece of metal money

coke **1** black stuff that is made from coal and can be burnt instead of coal
2 a brown, fizzy drink

cold **1** like ice or snow feels
2 an illness that makes you sneeze and blow your nose a lot

collage a picture made from small pieces of paper and material

collapse **1** to fall to pieces *The shed collapsed in the strong wind.*
2 to fall down because you are ill *The old lady collapsed on the floor.*

collar **1** the part that goes round the neck of clothes such as shirts and jackets
2 a band put round the neck of a dog or cat

collect **1** to bring things together from different places *I collect foreign coins.*
2 to go and get someone or something *She collected the children from school.*

collection **1** a set of things that have been collected *a stamp collection*
2 money collected from many people for a special reason

collector someone who collects things as a hobby or as a job

college **1** a kind of school
2 a place where people can carry on learning about something when they are too old for school

collide to hit someone or something by accident, while you are moving

collie a long-haired sheep dog

colliery a coal mine

colon a mark like this

collision a crash between two moving things

colour **1** red, blue, and green are colours
2 to use paint or crayon on something

colt a young, male horse

column **1** things on a list each below the other
2 a thick stone post that supports something or decorates a building *Nelson's Column*

comb **1** a strip of plastic, wood, or metal with a row of thin parts like teeth, for making hair tidy
2 to search a place very carefully *Police combed the area for the lost child.*

combine to join or mix together

combine-harvester a machine that cuts down corn and gets the seed out of it

combine-harvester

come **1** to move here *I came as soon as I could.*
2 to arrive *Has the letter come yet?*

comedian someone who entertains people by making them laugh

comedy a funny play

comfortable pleasant to be in, to sit on, or to wear *a comfortable chair*

comic **1** funny
2 a paper with stories told in pictures

comma a mark like this

command **1** to tell someone to do something *The captain was in command.*
2 to be in charge of something

common **1** usual *a common illness*
2 a piece of land that anyone can use

commotion a lot of noise *There was a great commotion when a dog ran into the school assembly.*

communication **1** a message
2 a way of sending or getting a message

community the people living in one place

companion a friend who is with you

company **1** having an animal or another person with you so that you are not lonely *The cat kept her company.*
2 a group of people who do things together *a company of actors*

compare to try to see how like each other some things are

compass an instrument that always shows where north is. A compass helps you to find your way when you are lost.

compasses an instrument for drawing circles *a pair of compasses*

compete to take part in a race or competition

competition a kind of test or game with a prize for the person who wins

complain to say that you are not pleased about something

complete **1** whole, with nothing missing *The jigsaw is complete – all the pieces are there.*
2 to come to the end of something

complicated **1** with a lot of different parts *a complicated machine*
2 difficult *a complicated sum*

compliment words that praise the person you are speaking to or writing to *She was paid a compliment when they said her dancing was excellent.*

composer someone who writes music

composition a story you have made up and written down

computer a machine which stores information on tape or disk, organizes it and then produces it when someone needs it

computer

conceal to hide *The money was concealed under the floor.*

conceited too proud of yourself and what you can do

concentrate to think hard about one thing

concern **1** to be important or interesting to someone or something *The information about the school trip concerned everyone.*
2 *concerned* worried

conjuror

concert an entertainment with music

concrete a mixture of cement and sand used for making buildings, paths, and bridges

condense to make something smaller.

condition the state something is in
The road surface is in poor condition.

conductor **1** someone who sells tickets on a bus and looks after the passengers *This bus doesn't have a conductor; you have to pay the driver.*
2 someone who stands facing a band, choir, or orchestra and keeps everyone playing together

cone **1** the shape of a witch's hat or an ice-cream cornet
2 a case for seeds on evergreen trees *a fir cone*

confess to say that you have done something wrong *He confessed to breaking the window.*

confetti tiny pieces of coloured paper that are thrown over a bride and bridegroom

confident **1** brave and not afraid *a confident swimmer*
2 sure about something *She was confident she knew the way.*

confuse to mix up *He always confuses the names of the twins.*

congratulate to tell someone how pleased you are about something special that has happened to them

conjuror someone who entertains people by doing tricks that look like magic

conker the hard, shiny brown nut that grows on a horse-chestnut tree

connect to join together *She connected the hose to the tap.*

conquer to beat in a battle or war

conscious (*say* kon-shuss) awake and able to understand what is happening around you
After the operation he slowly became conscious.

conservation taking good care of the world's air, water, plants, and animals

consider to think carefully about something

considerable large *a considerable amount of money*

considerate kind and thoughtful in the way you behave towards other people

consonant any letter of the alphabet except a e i o u and sometimes y

constable an ordinary policeman or policewoman

constellation a group of stars that form pictures or patterns in the sky

construct to build

contain to have something inside *The box contained toys.*

container anything that you can put other things into. Buckets, cups, bags, boxes, and jars are all containers.

contented happy with what you have

contents what is inside a container or a book *Be careful – the contents of this box are very fragile.*

contest a competition

continent one of the seven very large areas of land in the world

continue to go on doing something *They continued the game after lunch.*

contradict to say that someone is saying something that is not true *The teacher contradicted the child who said that the earth was flat.*

control to be in charge of something and be able to make it do what you want

convenient easy to get at or use

convent a place where nuns live and work together

conversation talking and listening to another person

convict a criminal who is in prison

convince to make someone believe something *He convinced her that ghosts were not real.*

cook **1** to get food ready to eat by heating it
2 someone whose job is to cook

cookery cooking food

cool not warm *a cool drink*

copper a shiny brown or red metal used for making pipes and coins

copy **1** to write down or draw what is already written down or drawn *She copied the poem in her best writing.*
2 to do exactly the same as someone else *She always copies what I wear.*

coral a kind of rock made in the sea from the bodies of tiny creatures. Coral can be many colours.

cord thin rope

core the part in the middle of something *an apple core*

corgi a kind of light brown dog with very short legs and pointed ears

cork The bark of a special kind of oak tree. It is put into the top of a bottle to close it.

corkscrew a tool for getting corks out of bottles

corn grain

corner the point where two edges or streets meet

cornet a wafer shaped like a cone, for holding ice-cream

cornflakes a kind of food made from corn, eaten with milk at breakfast

coronation the time when someone is crowned as king or queen

corpse a dead body

correct without any mistakes

corridor a long, narrow passage inside a big building or train. It has doors along it and people go down it to get from one room to another.

cost to have a certain price *The bike cost £100*

costume **1** clothes worn on the stage
2 clothes like ones worn long ago

cosy warm and comfortable

cottage a small house in the country

cotton **1** thread for sewing
2 a light cloth made from a plant that grows in hot countries *a cool cotton dress*

coral

cotton wool soft, white, fluffy, cotton stuff. Cotton wool is used in looking after babies and injured people and in packing delicate things.

couch a settee or sofa

cough to make a sudden, loud noise to get rid of something in your throat. Smoke and bad colds make people cough.

could   see can

council   a group of people chosen to plan and decide what should be done in a place   *a City Council*

count   **1** to say the numbers in order
2 to use numbers to find out how many people or things there are in a place

counter   **1** the long table where you are served in a shop, cafeteria, or bank
2 a small, round, flat piece of plastic used for playing some games

country   **1** a land with its own people and laws. England, Australia, and China are all countries.
2 the countryside

countryside   land with farms and villages, away from towns

crabs

county   one of the large areas Britain and Ireland are divided into

couple   two   *a couple of sweets*

coupon   a kind of ticket that you can change for a free gift. Some coupons make you able to buy things for less money than usual.

courage   the ability to be brave

course   **1** the direction something takes   *a ship's course*
2 a piece of ground where some kinds of sport take place
3 a series of lessons   *a swimming course*

court   **1** a piece of ground marked out for a game like netball or tennis
2 the place where a king or queen is living and the people who are with them
3 the place where people decide whether someone is guilty of breaking the law

cousin   the child of your aunt or uncle

cover   **1** to put one thing over or round another thing
2 something used for covering things

coward   someone who is afraid when they ought to be brave

cowboy   a man who rides round looking after the cattle on large farms in America

cowslip   a yellow wild flower that grows in the spring

crab   an animal with a shell, claws, and ten legs that lives in or near the sea

crack   **1** to make the sudden, sharp noise a dry twig makes when you snap it
2 a line on the surface of something where it has been partly broken. Cracks can come in walls, ceilings, cups, and plates.

cracker   **1** a paper tube with a toy and paper hat inside. It bangs when two people pull it apart.
Christmas crackers
2 a thin biscuit that is not sweet

crackle   to make the cracking sounds burning wood makes

cradle   a baby's bed

craftsman   someone who is very good at doing difficult work with their hands

crafty   clever at planning things so that you get your own way

crane   **1** a machine on wheels for lifting very heavy things
2 a large bird with very long legs

crash 1 the loud noise made when something heavy is dropped and smashed
2 to hit something with a loud noise *The car crashed into a tree.*

crate a container for carrying bottles or other things that break easily

crawl 1 to move on your hands and knees
2 to move slowly *The car crawled along in the fog.*
3 a way of swimming

crayon 1 a stick of coloured wax used for drawing
2 a coloured pencil

crazy likely to do strange or silly things

creak to make a loud, rough, squeaking noise. New shoes, doors that need oiling, and old wooden stairs creak.

cream 1 the thick part on the top of milk
2 the colour of cream
3 something that looks like cream and is put on the skin *hand-cream*

crease to make a line in something by folding it

create to make something no one else has made or can make *The sculptor created a new statue.*

creator someone who makes what no one else has made or can make

creature any animal

credit card a piece of plastic with your name and a number on it, which lets you buy goods that you need now and pay for them later

creek a small stream

creep 1 to move along, keeping close to the ground
2 to move quietly or secretly *We crept away and nobody saw us.*

crêpe paper (*say* krape paper) thin, coloured paper that you can stretch

crept see **creep**

crescent a street shaped like a curved line

cress a small, green plant that is eaten raw

crew a group of people who work together on a boat or aeroplane

cricket 1 a game played in a field by two teams with a ball, two bats, and two wickets
2 an insect that makes a shrill sound

cried see **cry**

crime an activity such as stealing which is against the law

criminal someone who has done something bad that is against the law

crimson a deep red colour

crinkle to make small lines in skin or paper by creasing it

cripple someone whose legs or arms are hurt so that they cannot use them properly

crisp 1 very dry so that it breaks easily
2 firm and fresh *a very crisp apple*
3 a very thin, dry slice of fried potato *a packet of crisps*

criss-cross with lines that cross each other

croak to make the hoarse sound a frog makes

crocodile a large reptile that lives in rivers in some hot countries. It has short legs, a long body, and sharp teeth.

crocodile

crocus a small white, yellow, or purple spring flower

crook **1** someone who cheats or robs people
2 a shepherd's stick with a curved top

crooked not straight

crystals (1)

crop **1** plants grown on a farm for food
2 to bite off the tops of plants. Sheep crop grass.

cross **1** to move across something
2 a mark like this + or ×
3 the shape of + or ×
4 angry

crouch to lean forwards and bend your knees so that your bottom is almost touching the ground

crow a big, black bird

crowd a large number of people

crown a big ring of silver or gold worn on the head by a king or queen

cruel very unkind

cruise to sail about without hurrying

crumb a tiny bit of bread or cake

crumble to break or fall into small pieces

crumple to make something very creased *crumpled clothes*

crunch to eat with the noise you make when you eat crisps

crush to damage something by pressing it hard

crust the hard part round the outside of bread

crutch a wooden stick that a crippled person can lean on when they are walking. It fits under their arm. *a pair of crutches*

cry **1** to let tears fall from your eyes *He was so upset that he cried.*
2 to shout

crystal **1** a hard material like very bright glass
2 the shape of snowflakes

cub a young bear, lion, tiger, or wolf

Cub Scout a junior Scout

cube the shape of dice or sugar lumps. Cubes have six square sides that are all the same size.

cuckoo a bird that lays its eggs in other birds' nests. The male cry sounds like *cuck-oo.*

cucumber a long, green vegetable eaten raw

cuddle to put your arms closely round a person or animal that you love

cuff the part joined to the end of a sleeve to fit round the wrist

cul-de-sac a street closed at one end *We live in a quiet cul-de-sac.*

culprit the person who is guilty

cunning crafty

cupboard a piece of furniture or a space inside a wall. Cupboards have doors and usually some shelves.

cure to make well again

curiosity a wish to find out about things

curious **1** wanting to know about something *She was curious to know what her present would be.*
2 unusual *a curious smell*

curl **1** a piece of hair twisted into rings
2 *to curl up* to sit or lie comfortably with the body bent round itself

cymbals

cymbals a musical instrument that is two round pieces of metal that you bang together *a pair of cymbals*

cypress a kind of tree. It has dark leaves that it keeps all through the year.

D d

currant a small, black, dried grape

current water, air, or electricity moving in one direction

curry a cooked food with a spicy flavour

curtain a piece of cloth pulled in front of a window or stage to cover it

curtsy to put one foot behind the other and bend the knees. Women and girls curtsy. *She curtsied to the Queen.*

curve a line that is bent smoothly like the letter C

cushion a cloth bag filled with soft material so that it is comfortable to sit on or rest against

custard a thick, sweet, yellow liquid poured over puddings

custom something that is usually done. It is a custom to give Christmas presents.

customer someone who uses a shop or a bank

cut **1** to use scissors or a knife to open, divide, or shape something *She's cutting out the picture. I've cut up your meat for you.* **2** an opening in the skin made by something sharp

cutlery knives, forks, and spoons

cycle to ride a bicycle

cygnet (*say* sig-nit) a young swan

cylinder the shape of a tin of soup or a toilet roll

dachshund a kind of dog with very short legs and a long body

daffodil a yellow flower that grows from a bulb

daft silly

dagger a very short sword with two sharp edges

daily every day

dairy **1** a place where milk is made into butter and cheese **2** a shop that sells milk, cream, butter, and cheese

daisy a small flower with white petals and a yellow centre

dale a valley

dam a wall built to hold water back. Some dams are built to stop floods happening.

damage to harm something *The rain damaged the wheat in the field.*

damp a little wet *damp grass*

damson a small, dark purple plum

dance to move about in time to music

dandelion a yellow wild flower with a thick stalk

danger **1** something that is dangerous **2** the chance of something dangerous happening *danger of fire*

dangerous likely to kill or harm you *It's dangerous to play in the road.*

dangle to hang loosely *He saw his scarf dangling from the branch.*

dare **1** to be brave enough or rude enough to do something   *I daren't dive in. How dare you!*
2 to ask someone to show how brave they are   *I dare you to climb that tree.*

daring   very brave

dark **1** without any light   *a dark house*
2 not light in colour   *a dark green coat*

darling   someone who is loved very much

darn   to sew over a hole in a garment to mend it

dart **1** to move very quickly and suddenly
2 something with a sharp point that you throw at a target

dash **1** to move very quickly
2 a mark like this –

data **1** facts or information
2 information that is being worked on by the program in a computer

date **1** the day, the month, and the year when something happens
2 a sweet, brown fruit that grows on a palm tree

dates 2

daughter   a girl or woman who is someone's child

dawdle   to walk too slowly   *He was late for school because he was dawdling.*

dawn   the time of the day when the sun rises

day **1** the twenty-four hours between midnight and the next midnight
2 the part of the day when it is light

dazed   not able to think properly. People are often dazed after an accident.

dazzle   to be so bright that it hurts your eyes to look   *The sun was dazzling.*

dead   not alive

deaf   not able to hear

deal **1** to give out   *I dealt the cards.*
2 *to deal with something* to do a job that needs doing
3 *a great deal* a lot

dealt   (*say* delt)
see **deal**

dear **1** loved. Dear is always used to begin letters, for example   *Dear Tom . . .*
2 costing a lot   *butter is dear*

death   the end of life

debt   something that you owe someone

decay   to go bad   *Sugar makes teeth decay.*

deceit   making someone believe something that is not true

deceive   to make someone believe something that is not true   *They deceived the bus conductor, saying they had already paid.*

decide   to make up your mind about something

decimal **1** using tens   *the decimal system*
2 a way of writing fractions by putting numbers after a dot. $^3/_{10}$ is 0.3 $^1/_2$ is 0.5

decision   what you have decided

deck   a floor on a ship or bus

declare   to say something important that you want everyone to know   *The mayor declared the fête open.*

decorate   to make something look pretty

decrease   to make smaller or fewer   *She decreased the number of stitches on her knitting-needles.*

deed something special that someone has done *a good deed*

deep going a long way down from the top *deep water, a deep hole*

deer a graceful animal that can move very quickly. Male deer have big horns like branches growing out of their heads. *two deer*

deer

defeat to beat someone in a game or battle

defend to keep someone or something safe from attack *The soldiers defended the castle.*

definite fixed or certain *a definite date for the holiday*

defy to say or show that you will not obey

degree a measurement for temperature. You can write it like this °, and so ten degrees is 10 °.

delay 1 to make someone or something late
2 to put off doing something until later

deliberate done on purpose *a deliberate mistake*

delicate 1 soft and fine *delicate material*
2 likely to get ill or damaged *a delicate child delicate machinery*

delicious tasting or smelling very pleasant

delight to please very much *The surprise gift delighted her.*

deliver 1 to bring things like milk or newspapers to someone's house
2 to set free

delivery delivering something

demand to ask for something that you think you ought to have *He demanded his money back.*

demolish to knock something down and break it up

demonstrate to show *She's demonstrating how it works.*

demonstration a lot of people marching through the streets to show everyone what they think about something

dense thick *a dense fog, a dense forest*

dent to make a hollow in something hard, by hitting it. Cars are often dented in accidents.

dentist someone whose job is to look after teeth. He can take out bad teeth or fill them.

deny to say that something is not true *She denied breaking the cup.*

depart to go away

depend to trust someone or something to give you the help you need *The blind man depends on his guide dog.*

depress to make someone feel sad

depth how deep something is

descend (*say* di-<u>send</u>) to go down

describe to say what something or someone is like

description words that tell you about someone or something

desert (*say* <u>dez</u>-ert) dry land where very few plants can grow

deserted left by everyone *a deserted house*

deserve to have done something that makes people think you should get a reward or a punishment *He was so brave he deserves a medal.*

design to draw a plan or pattern for something

desire to want very much

desk a kind of table where you can read, write, and keep books

despair to give up hope *She despaired of learning Chinese.*

desperate ready to do even dangerous or stupid things, because you have lost hope *a desperate robber*

despise to dislike someone because they are bad and you think you are much better than they are *They despised him because he had cheated.*

dessert (*say* di-zert) sweet food eaten after the main part of a meal

destination the place you are travelling to

destroy 1 to damage something so badly that it cannot be used again 2 to kill a very sick animal that cannot be cured

destroyer a small, fast ship for attacking other ships

destruction when something is destroyed

detail a tiny piece of information about something *She could remember every detail about the house.*

detective someone who tries to find out who did a murder or robbery

determined with your mind firmly made up *determined to win*

detest to hate

develop to become bigger or better

device something that has been made for a special purpose *A can-opener is a useful device.*

dew tiny drops of water that form during the night on things outside

diagonal a slanting line drawn from one corner of something to the opposite corner

diagram a kind of picture that explains something *The car book had a diagram of an engine.*

diagram of a car engine

dial a circle with numbers or letters round it. Clocks, watches, and telephones have dials.

dialect the way people living in a particular place speak

diameter the distance across a circle, through the centre

diamond 1 a very hard jewel like clear glass 2 a shape with four sloping sides that are the same length. Some playing-cards have red diamonds printed on them.

diary a book where you can write down what happens every day

dice a small cube used in games. Each side is marked with a different number of spots from 1 to 6.

dictionary a book where you can find out what a word means and how to spell it

did see do

die to stop living *The dog was dying. The king had died.*

diet special meals that some people must have to be healthy

difference how different one thing is from another thing

different not like someone or something else

difficult not easy *a difficult sum*

difficulty 1 something difficult
2 *with difficulty* not easily

dig to move soil away to make a hole in the ground *I dug a hole and planted the tree.*

digest to change the food in your stomach so your body can use it

dignified looking serious and important *The mayor looked dignified.*

dim not bright

dimple a small hollow in the cheek or chin

dinghy (*say* ding-ee) a small boat

dingy (*say* din-jee) looking dirty *a dingy room*

dining-room the room where people have their meals

dinner the main meal of the day

dinosaur a large animal that lived millions of years ago

direct 1 to show someone the way
2 as straight and quick as it can be *the direct route*

direction the way you go to get somewhere

dirt dust or mud

dirty marked with dirt or stains *a dirty face*

disagree to think that someone else is wrong and you are right

disappear to go away and not be seen any more

disappoint to make someone sad by not doing what they hoped

disaster something very bad that happens suddenly

disc any round, flat object
I have a collection of music discs.

discs

disciple a follower of a great teacher or a religious leader

discourage to try to stop someone doing something by telling them how difficult or foolish it is *They discouraged him from rock-climbing.*

discover to find out about something

discovery finding out about something

discuss to talk about something with people who have different ideas about it

disease illness

disgraceful so bad that it brings you shame *disgraceful work*

disguise to make yourself look different so that people will not recognize you *The thief disguised himself as a policeman.*

disgust to be so nasty that people hate it

dishonest not honest

disk a device for storing a lot of data for a computer

disk drive a device for reading a computer disk in the same way that a turntable plays a record

disk drive

disk drive

dislike to feel that you do not like someone or something

dismal dark and sad *The weather was dismal – cold, wet, and grey.*

dismay to make someone lose hope and be afraid *He was dismayed to find he was still lost and it was nearly night.*

dismiss to send someone away *The teacher dismissed the class at the end of the day.*

display 1 to show *The class displayed their work.*
2 a show *a dancing display*

dissolve to mix something into a liquid so that it becomes part of the liquid. You can dissolve salt in water very easily.

distance the amount of space between two places *The teacher asked the children to estimate the distance between the two trees.*

distant far away

distinct 1 easy to see or hear *The cuckoo call was quite distinct.*
2 different *Each type of pig has distinct colours.*

distress great sorrow, trouble, or worry

district part of a town, city, county, or country

disturb 1 to upset someone's peace or rest
2 to move something out of place

disturbance something that upsets someone's peace or rest

ditch a long, narrow hole. Ditches are dug to take away water from land.

divan a low bed

dive to jump head first into water

divide 1 to share something out
2 to split something into smaller parts
3 to find out how many times one number goes into another. Six divided by two is three, $6 \div 2 = 3$.

divorce the ending of a marriage

dizzy feeling as if everything is spinning round you

do 1 to carry out an action *She does her sewing neatly. Don't cry. What are you doing?*
2 to finish *I did my work before I went out to play. He didn't. Have you done your picture yet?*

dock a place where ships and boats are loaded, unloaded, or mended

doctor someone whose job is to help sick people to get better

dodge to move quickly to get out of the way of something

doe a female deer, rabbit, or hare

does see **do**

doll a toy in the shape of a person

dollar an amount of money. Dollars are used in the United States of America, Australia, and some other countries.

dolphin an animal with warm blood that lives in the sea

dolphin

dome a roof shaped like the top half of a ball. St. Paul's Cathedral has a dome.

domino a small, oblong piece of wood or plastic with spots on it. You use twenty-eight dominoes to play the game called **dominoes**

done see **do**

donkey an animal that looks like a small horse with long ears

doodle to scribble while you are thinking about something else

dose the amount of medicine someone has to take

double twice as much or as many

doubt (*rhymes with* out)
the feeling you have when you are not sure about something

doubtful not sure

dough (*rhymes with* so)
a mixture of flour and water. Dough is used for making bread and cakes.

doughnut a small cake that is fried and covered in sugar

dove a bird that looks like a small pigeon

down **1** to somewhere lower *Run down the hill.*
2 very soft feathers

downward, downwards
moving to somewhere lower

doze to be nearly asleep

dozen a set of twelve

drab looking dull *drab clothes*

drag to pull something heavy along

dragon a monster with wings, that you read about in stories. Dragons breathe out fire and often guard treasure.

dragon

dragonfly a brightly coloured insect that lives near water

drain **1** a pipe for taking away water
2 to get rid of water by using pipes or ditches

drake a male duck

drama   acting in a play or story

drank   see **drink**

draught   (*rhymes with* raft)
1 cold air that blows into a room
2 one of twenty-four round pieces used in the game of **draughts**

draw   1 to do a picture with a pen, pencil, or crayon
2 to end a game with the same score as the other side   *They drew 1–1 last Saturday.*

drawbridge   a bridge over the water round a castle. It can be pulled up to stop people getting into the castle.

drawer   a box without a lid, that slides into a piece of furniture

drawn   see **draw**

dread   great fear   *Cats have a dread of water.*

dreadful   very bad   *dreadful weather*

dream   to see and hear things while you are asleep   *Last night I dreamt about Christmas.*

drench   to make someone very wet all over   *He was drenched by the rain.*

dress   1 to put clothes on
2 a piece of clothing that is like a skirt and blouse in one

drew   see **draw**

dribble   1 to let liquid come out of your mouth without meaning to. Babies often dribble.
2 to keep kicking a ball as you run along, so that the ball stays close to your feet   *He dribbled the ball a little way and then passed.*

drift   to be carried gently along by water or air

drill   a tool for making holes

drink   to swallow liquid   *Have you drunk your milk?   He was thirsty so he drank a lot.*

drip   to let drops of liquid fall off

drive   to make a machine or animal move   *He's never driven a bus before. I drove the cows into the field.   He was driving too fast.*

drizzle   very light rain

droop   to hang down weakly   *a drooping flower*

drop   1 a tiny amount of liquid   *a drop of blood*
2 to let something fall

drove   see **drive**

drown   to die because you are under water and cannot breathe

drowsy   sleepy

drum   a hollow musical instrument that you bang with a stick

drums

drunk   see **drink**

dry   not damp or wet   *dry land*

duchess   a woman married to a duke

duck   1 a bird that lives near water. It has a wide, flat beak
2 to bend down quickly to get out of the way

due   1 expected   *The train is due now.*
2 *due to* caused by   *The accident was due to the fog.*

duel   a fight between two people using the same kind of weapon   *a duel with swords*

duffel-coat a thick coat with a hood and long, narrow buttons that go through loops

dug see **dig**

duke a very important nobleman

dull 1 not interesting *a dull book*
2 not bright *a dull colour*
3 not sharp *a dull sound*

dumb not able to speak

dummy 1 a piece of rubber made for a baby to suck
2 a model of a person. You often see dummies in shop windows.

dump 1 a place where rubbish is left
2 to leave something you want to get rid of
3 to put something down carelessly *She dumped her school-bag on the table.*

dungeon (*say* dunjun) a prison underneath a building

during while something else is going on *I fell asleep during the film.*

dusk the dim light at the end of the day, before it gets dark

dust 1 dry dirt that is like powder
2 to clear dust away from something

dustbin a large container with a lid, for rubbish

duty what you ought to do *A soldier's duty is to fight for his country.*

duvet (*say* doovay) a cover for a bed instead of blankets

dwarf a very small person in a fairy story

dwindle to get smaller and smaller *The crowd dwindled away once the rain started.*

dye to change the colour of something by putting it in a special liquid *He dyed his hair orange.*

dying see **die**

dynamite something very powerful that is used for blowing things up *a stick of dynamite*

E e

each every *Each child had a cake.*

eager full of a strong wish to do something *They were eager to start the race.*

eagle a large bird that eats other animals

ear 1 the part of the head used for hearing
2 the group of seeds at the top of a stalk of corn

early 1 near the beginning *early in the day*
2 sooner than we expected *She came early.*

earn to get money by working for it

earth 1 the planet that we all live on
2 soil

earthquake a time when the ground suddenly shakes. Strong earthquakes can destroy buildings.

ease rest from pain and trouble

easel a stand for holding a blackboard or a picture while you work at it

east in the direction of the rising sun

Easter the day when Christians specially remember that Jesus Christ came back from the dead

eastern from the east or in the east

easy 1 able to be done or understood without any trouble *an easy sum*
2 comfortable *an easy chair*

eat to take food into the body *Has he eaten his dinner? He ate it all five minutes ago.*

47

eccentric   likely to behave in a strange way   *The eccentric man kept a fly as a pet.*

echo   a sound that is heard again as it bounces back off something solid. Echoes are often heard in caves and tunnels.

eclipse   **1** a time when the moon comes between the earth and the sun so that the sun's light cannot be seen   **2** a time when the earth comes between the sun and the moon so that the moon's light cannot be seen

eclipse 1

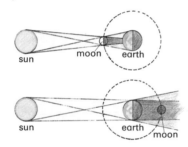

sun   moon   earth

sun   earth   moon

eclipse 2

edge   the part along the end or side of something

edit   **1** to get a newspaper, magazine, or book ready for printing   **2** to put a story, film, or tape-recording in the order you want

editor   the person in charge of a newspaper, magazine, or comic. Editors decide which stories and pictures will be printed.

education   the teaching and training people get in schools and colleges

eel   a fish that looks like a snake

effect   anything that happens because of something else   *The effect of the snow was that the roads were blocked.*

effort   hard work at something you are trying to do

egg   **1** an oval object with a thin shell, made by a hen and used as food   **2** one of the oval objects that baby birds, fish, insects, or snakes live inside until they are big enough to be born

eiderdown   a large, cloth bag filled with something soft like feathers and used as a cover for a bed

either   one or the other of two people or things   *It's either right or wrong.*

elastic   a strip of material that can stretch in length and then go back to its usual size

elbow   the bony part in the middle of the arm where it bends

elder   older than another person   *She is the elder of the two sisters.*

election   a time when people can choose the men and women who will be in charge of their town or country   *a General Election*

electric   worked by electricity

electricity   power that moves along wires. Electricity is used for giving light and heat and for making machines work.

electron   something very tiny that carries electricity

electronic   worked by electrons

elephant   a very big grey animal with tusks and a very long nose called a trunk, that it uses like an arm

elf   a kind of fairy   *two elves*

elm   a kind of tall tree

else   besides   *Ask someone else.*

embark   to get on a ship at the beginning of a journey

embarrass   to make someone feel shy and upset

embrace   to put your arms round someone

embroidery   pretty sewing that decorates something

emerald   a green jewel

emergency   something very dangerous that suddenly happens

emigrate   to go and live in another country

emperor   a man who rules over a group of countries

empire   a group of countries ruled over by one person

employ   to pay someone to work for you

empress   **1** a woman who rules over a group of countries
2 the wife of an emperor

empty   with nothing in it or on it

enamel   **1** a kind of paint that gives a hard, shiny surface to things
2 the hard, shiny surface of your teeth

encourage   to make someone brave and full of hope so that they will do something   *He encouraged her to dive from the diving-board.*

elephants

encyclopedia   a book or set of books that tells you about all kinds of things

end   **1** the last part of something
2 to finish

endeavour   to try hard

enemy   **1** someone who wants to hurt you
2 the people fighting on the other side

energetic   full of the strength for doing a lot of things

energy   the strength to do things

engine   a machine that makes its own power and is used to make things move

engineer   someone who plans the building of roads, bridges, or machines

enjoy   to like watching, listening to, or doing something

enormous   very big

enough   as much as is needed   *enough money*

enter   **1** to come or go in
2 to take part in a race or a competition

entertain   to make time pass very pleasantly for people   *The clown entertained the children.*

entertainment   anything that entertains people. Shows, circuses, plays, and films are entertainments.

enthusiasm   a very great interest in something   *an enthusiasm for football*

enthusiastic   so interested in something that you spend a lot of time on it and are always talking about it

entire   whole   *The entire class was ill.*

entrance   the way into a place

entry   **1** a way into a place   *the entry to the tunnel*
2 going or coming into a place   *A 'No Entry' sign.*
3 a person, animal, or thing in a competition   *There were many entries for the show cat competition.*

envelope   a paper cover for a letter

envious   full of envy

environment everything around you that affects how you live and develop *Pollution is a danger to the environment*

envy a feeling you get when you would like to have something that someone else has

equal the same as something else in amount, size, or value *They had equal shares of the cake.*

equator an imaginary line round the middle of the earth. Countries near the equator are very hot.

equipment the things you need for doing something

erect upright

errand a short journey to take a message or fetch something for someone

error a mistake

escalator a moving staircase

escalator

escape **1** to get free *The prisoner escaped.*
2 to get away *They escaped from the rain by going into a café.*

Eskimo (*also called* Innuit) one of the people who live in very cold parts of North America, Greenland, and Russia

especially more than anything else

estate **1** an area of land with a lot of houses on it *a housing estate*
2 a large area of land that belongs to one person

estimate to guess the amount, size, or price

ethnic about one particular race or group of people

eve the day or night before a special day *Christmas Eve*

even **1** level or equal *Our scores were even.*
2 that two will go into *Six is an even number.*

evening the time at the end of the day before people go to bed

event something important that happens *Your birthday is an important event.*

eventually in the end

ever **1** at any time *Have you ever read this?*
2 *for ever* always

evergreen any tree that has green leaves all through the year

every each *Every week has seven days.*

everybody, everyone every person

everything all things

everywhere in all places

evil very wicked *an evil deed*

ewe (*say* you) a female sheep

exact just right

exaggerate to make something sound bigger than it is *He exaggerated the size of the fish he caught.*

exam, examination an important test

examine to look at something very carefully

example **1** anything that shows how something works or what it is like *The class copied the example from the book.*
2 a person or thing that should be copied *He behaves so well he sets a good example.*

excellent very good

except apart from *Everyone got a prize except me.*

exchange to give something and get something in return

excite to interest someone so much that they have strong feelings such as love, fear, or anger *an exciting film*

excitement an excited feeling

exclaim to make a sudden sound because you are surprised or excited

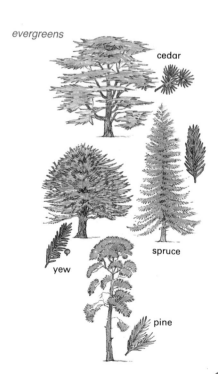

evergreens

cedar

spruce

yew

pine

exclamation mark a mark like this !
put after words to show that they have been shouted or are surprising

excursion a trip out somewhere for the day or afternoon *an excursion to the seaside*

excuse¹ *(ends in the sound —s)*
words that try to explain why you have done wrong so that you will not get into trouble *Her excuse for being late was that she had missed the bus.*

excuse² *(ends in the sound —z)*
to forgive

execute to kill someone as a punishment *In some countries murderers are executed.*

exercise **1** work that makes your body healthy and strong *Take exercise to keep fit.*
2 a piece of work that you do to make yourself better at something *Do this exercise to practise your handwriting.*

exhausted tired out

exhibition a group of things put on show so that people can come to see them *an exhibition of paintings*

exile someone who has to live away from their own country

exist **1** to be real, not imaginary *Do fairies exist?*
2 to live

exit the way out of a place

expand to get bigger. A balloon expands when you blow air into it.

expect to think something is very likely to happen *It is so cold I expect it will snow.*

expedition a journey made in order to do something *a climbing expedition*

expensive with a high price *an expensive car*

experience **1** what you have learnt from things that you have seen and done *The experience of living on a farm has made him fond of all animals.* **2** something that has happened to you *a frightening experience*

experiment a test to find out whether an idea works

an experiment

expert someone who does something very well or knows a lot about something

explain to make something clear to people so that they understand it

explanation something said or written to help people to understand

explode to make something burst or blow up with a loud bang *Bombs explode.*

explore to look carefully round a place for the first time

explosion a loud bang made by something bursting or blowing up

explosive anything used for making things blow up

express **1** a fast train **2** to put an idea or feeling into words *He expressed his regret that he could not help.*

expression the look on someone's face

extension a part that has been added to make something bigger *a kitchen extension.*

extent the length or area of something *The train set covered the full extent of the bedroom floor.*

extinguish to put out a fire

extra more than usual

extraordinary very unusual

extravagant always ready to spend much more money than people think you ought

extreme **1** very great *extreme cold* **2** the furthest away *the extreme north*

eye **1** the part of the head used for seeing **2** the small hole in a needle

eye

eyebrow the curved line of hair above each eye

eyelash one of the short hairs that grow in a fringe around each eye

Ff

fable a story about animals that teaches people something

face **1** the front part of the head **2** a surface *A cube has six faces.* **3** to have the front towards something *The church is facing the school.*

fact anything that people know is true

factory a building where machines are used to make things

fade **1** to lose colour *faded curtains*
2 to get paler or quieter so that it is harder to see or hear *The music faded at the end of the tape.*

Fahrenheit (*say* farren-hite) a way of measuring temperature that gives 32 degrees for freezing water and 212 degrees for boiling water

fail to try to do something but not be able to do it

failure someone or something that has failed

faint **1** weak *a faint cry*
2 to feel so dizzy that everything goes black and you fall down

fair **1** light in colour *fair hair*
2 right or just *It's not fair.*
3 a group of roundabouts, stalls, shows, and games that are set up in a place for a few days

fair 3

fairly **1** without cheating *Play fairly.*
2 almost or quite *fairly good, I'm fairly sure.*

fairy one of the tiny, magic people in stories

faith belief in someone or something

faithful always ready to help your friends and do what you have promised to do

fake something not valuable that is made to look valuable *The painting was a fake.*

fall to come down suddenly *He's fallen off his bike. I fell over yesterday.*

false **1** not real *false teeth*
2 not true *a false friend*

falter **1** to keep stopping and nearly falling over *The baby faltered when she tried walking on her own.*
2 to keep stopping while you are speaking *Her voice faltered as she spoke to the large crowd.*

fame being famous *great fame*

familiar well known to you *a familiar face*

family parents and their children and grandchildren

famine a time when there is very little food

famous very well known

fancy **1** decorated *a fancy hat*
2 *fancy dress* unusual dressing-up clothes
3 to want *I fancied an ice-cream.*

fang a long, sharp tooth. Dogs, wolves, and poisonous snakes have fangs.

far a long way *far from home*

fare the money people have to pay to travel on trains, buses, boats, or aeroplanes

farewell goodbye

farm a piece of land where someone grows crops and keeps animals for food

farmer someone who keeps a farm

farther to a greater distance *I live farther away now.*

fashion   the up-to-date way of dressing most people like and try to copy

fast   **1** moving quickly   *a fast car*
2 quickly   *Don't drive too fast.*
3 firmly fixed   *It was stuck fast in the mud.*
4 showing a time that is later than the correct time. Watches and clocks are sometimes fast.
5 to have nothing to eat for a time

fasten   **1** to close something so that it will not come open   *Fasten the seat-belt.*
2 to join to something   *Fasten a label on the bag.*

fastener   something used for fastening things   *a zip-fastener*

fat   **1** with a very thick, round body
2 the white, greasy part of meat
3 any grease that is used in cooking. Butter, margarine, and lard are fats.

fatal   causing death   *a fatal accident*

father   a male parent

fault   something wrong that spoils a person or thing

favour   something kind that you do for someone

favourite   liked the most

fawn   **1** a young deer
2 a light brown colour

fawn 1

fear   **1** a feeling you get when you think something bad might happen to you
2 to be afraid of someone or something

feast   a special meal for a lot of people

feat   something brave or difficult that has been done   *Climbing the mountain was a daring feat.*

feather   one of the many light, flat parts that cover a bird instead of hair or fur

fed   see **feed**

feeble   weak

feed   **1** to give food to a person or animal   *I fed the cat last night.*
2 to eat   *The pigs are feeding now.*

feel   **1** to touch something to find out what it is like
2 to know something inside yourself

feeling   something that you feel inside yourself, like anger or love

feet   more than one **foot**

fell   see **fall**

felt   **1** see **feel**
2 a kind of cloth made from wool

female   any person or animal that can become a mother

feminist   someone who believes that women should have the same opportunities in life as men

fence   a kind of wall made of wood or posts and wire. Fences are put round gardens and fields.

fern   a plant with leaves like feathers and no flowers

ferret   a small animal used for catching rats and rabbits

ferret

ferry a boat that takes people from one side of a piece of water to the other

fertile able to make a lot of healthy plants *fertile soil*

festival a time when people do special things to show that they are happy about something

fetch to go and get

fête (*rhymes with* date) a kind of party in the open air with competitions and stalls selling different things *At the fête there was a lucky dip.*

fever an illness that makes people feel very hot and dizzy

few not many

fiddle 1 a violin
2 to play about with something *She fiddled with her pencil during the story.*

fidget to keep moving because you cannot keep still *The excited class fidgeted on the floor waiting for the news.*

field a piece of ground with a fence around it and crops or grass growing on it

fierce angry and cruel

fight to take part in a struggle, battle, or war

figure 1 one of the signs for numbers, such as 1, 2, and 3
2 the shape of a body

file 1 a line of people one behind the other *Line up in single file.*
2 a flat tool that is rubbed against things to make them smooth *A nail-file will keep your nails smooth.*

fill to make someone or something full

film 1 a piece or roll of thin plastic put in a camera for taking photographs
2 moving photographs with sound that tell a story

filthy very dirty

fin one of the thin, flat parts that stand out from a fish's body and help it swim

find to come across something, either by chance or because you have been looking for it *I've found my coat.*

fine 1 very thin *fine material*
2 dry and sunny *fine weather*
3 very good *a fine picture*
4 money someone has to pay as a punishment *a parking fine*

finger one of the five separate parts at the end of the hand

fingerprint the mark left on the surface of something by the tip of a finger

finish to come to the end of something

fir a tall tree that has cones and leaves that look like green needles

fire 1 the heat and bright light that come from burning things
2 *to fire a gun* to shoot

fireman a man whose job is to put out fires

fire-place the part of a room where the fire and hearth are

firework a paper tube filled with a powder that will burn noisily and bang or send out coloured sparks and smoke

firm fixed so that it will not give way

first before all the others

fish 1 any animal with scales and fins that always lives and breathes under water
2 to try to catch fish

film 1

flags

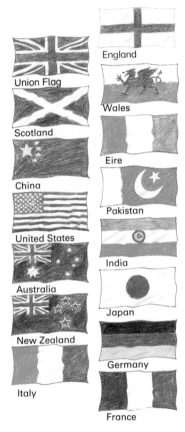

Union Flag

Scotland

China

United States

Australia

New Zealand

Italy

England

Wales

Eire

Pakistan

India

Japan

Germany

France

flag a piece of coloured cloth with a pattern on it, joined to a stick. Every country has its own flag.

flake a very thin, light piece of something *snowflakes*

flame fire that is shaped like a pointed tongue

flannel a piece of soft cloth used for washing yourself

flap **1** to move up and down like a bird's wings
2 a part that hangs down and is joined to the rest by one side. Envelopes have flaps.

flare to burn with a sudden, bright flame

flash to shine suddenly and brightly

flask a container that keeps hot drinks hot and cold drinks cold

flat **1** not curved and with no bumps in it *A snooker table must be perfectly flat.*
2 a home that is a set of rooms inside a house or a big building *a block of flats*

flatten to make flat *The field of corn was flattened by the strong wind.*

flatter to praise someone too much *She flattered the man, saying his cooking was the best she had eaten.*

flavour the smell and taste of something *Which flavour of ice-cream do you like?*

flea a small jumping insect without wings that sucks blood

flee to run away *He saw the policeman and fled.*

fleece the wool that covers a sheep

flesh the soft stuff between the bones and skin

flew see **fly**

flight **1** a journey through the air
2 an escape *They made their flight from the prison as soon as it was dark.*
3 *a flight of stairs* a set of stairs

fisherman someone who catches fish

fishmonger someone who keeps a shop that sells fish

fist a hand with all the fingers pressed in towards the palm

fit **1** healthy
2 good enough *fit for a king*
3 to be the right size and shape

fix **1** to join firmly to something *Fix the shelf onto the wall.*
2 to mend *She fixed the broken toy.*

fizzy with a lot of tiny bubbles that keep bursting *fizzy drinks*

flinch to move back slightly because you are afraid

fling to throw something as hard as you can *I flung a stone and hit the giant.*

float 1 to be on the top of a liquid *Wood floats on water.*
2 to be carried along by liquid or air *The balloon floated in the air.*

flock a group of birds or sheep that feed together

flood a lot of water that spreads over land that is usually dry

floor the part of a building or room that people walk on

flop to fall or sit down suddenly *After the race she flopped down to the ground.*

floppy disk a device for storing a large amount of information for a computer

flour a powder made from wheat and used for making bread, pastry, and cakes

flourish 1 to grow well *The plants flourished.*
2 to be happy and successful *The Brownie pack is flourishing. It is getting very popular.*

flow to move along like a river *The traffic was flowing smoothly on the motorway.*

flower the part of a plant that produces seeds

flown see **fly**

flu an illness that gives you a cold and makes you ache all over and feel very hot

fluff light, soft stuff that comes off wool, hair, or feathers

fluke a piece of luck that makes you able to do something you thought you could not do *He scored the goal by a lucky fluke.*

flung see **fling**

flutter 1 to keep moving the wings quickly, but not fly very far
2 to move a little, like a flag in a very light wind

fly 1 to move through the air with wings or in an aeroplane *I flew from London to Paris last week.*
He's never flown before.
2 a small insect with one pair of wings

foal a young horse

foal

foam 1 a lot of small bubbles on the top of a liquid
2 thick, soft rubber used for making sponges

fog damp air that looks like thick smoke and is difficult to see through

fold to lay one part of something on top of another part

folder a large cover made of card for keeping your work in

foliage leaves

folk people

follow to go after

fond liking someone or something a lot *fond of fish fingers*

food anything that you eat to help you grow and be healthy

fool someone who is very silly

foolish silly

foot **1** the part joined to the lower end of the leg *two feet*
2 a measure for length

football a game played by two teams who kick a ball and try to score goals

footprint the mark left by a foot

footsteps the sound your feet make as you walk or run

forbid to say that someone must not do something *She was forbidden to go out.*

force **1** to use your power to make a person, animal, or thing do something *The man forced open the door.*
2 a group of people with weapons
3 power *The force of his punch knocked out the other boxer.*

forecast saying what you think is going to happen before it happens *a weather forecast*

forehead the part of the face above the eyebrows

foreign belonging to another country *foreign coins*

forest a lot of trees growing together

forgave see **forgive**

forge **1** to write or paint like someone else to deceive people *She forged his signature.*
2 to make a copy of something and pretend it is real
3 a place where metal is heated and shaped *In the blacksmith's forge horseshoes are made.*

forgery writing or a picture that is made to look as if someone else has done it

forget to fail to remember *I've forgotten my dinner money. I forgot the time and was late.*

forgive to stop being angry with someone *Have you forgiven me? I forgave him when he explained.*

forgot, forgotten see **forget**

fork a tool with three or four thin, pointed parts. People use small forks for picking up food and putting it into their mouths.

form **1** the shape something has
2 a long wooden seat without a back
3 one of the classes in a school *I am in Form 2.*
4 a printed paper with spaces where you have to write *Fill in the form.*

fort a strong building with soldiers in it, made to protect a place against its enemies

fortnight two weeks

fortress a big fort

fortunate lucky

fortune **1** a lot of money *He won a fortune at bingo.*
2 luck *She set out to seek her fortune.*

forward, forwards in the direction you are facing

fossil any part of a dead plant or animal that has been in the ground millions of years and become hard like rock

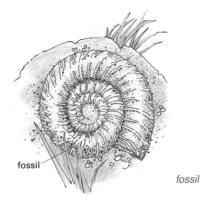

fossil

fossil

foster-mother a woman who takes a child to live with her family while the child's parents cannot look after them

fought see **fight**

foul   dirty and bad

found   see **find**

foundations   the solid part under the ground that a building is built on

fountain   water that shoots up into the air

fowl   any bird that is kept for its meat or eggs, like a hen

fox   a wild animal that looks like a dog and has a long, furry tail

fox

fraction   **1** a number that is not a whole number. ½, ⅗, and ¼ are fractions
2 a very small part of something

fragile   easily broken   *Glass is fragile.*

fragment   a small piece that has been broken off   *fragments of rock*

frame   something that fits round the edge of a picture

fraud   a trick or a person who tries to cheat someone

freak   any person, animal, or thing with something very strange about it

freckle   one of the small brown spots people sometimes get on their skin, when they have been in the sun

free   **1** with nothing to stop you doing something or going somewhere
2 not costing anything   *a free gift*

freeze   **1** to change into ice   *The pond froze last night.*
2 to be very cold   *Your hands will be frozen.*

freezer   a large refrigerator used for keeping food very cold for a long time

frequent   happening often   *frequent rain*

fresh   **1** not old, tired, or used   *fresh air, fresh bread, a fresh start*
2 not tinned   *fresh fruit*

fret   to keep worrying and getting upset about something   *The dog fretted when its owners went away.*

fridge   short for **refrigerator**

friend   someone you like who likes you. Friends like doing things together.

frieze   a wide strip of pictures along the top of a wall   *an alphabet frieze in the classroom*

fright   sudden fear

frighten   to make someone afraid

frill   a strip of material with tiny pleats in it. Frills are stitched to the edges of things to decorate them.

fringe   short hair brushed forward on to the forehead

fritter   a slice of potato, fruit, or meat dipped in a mixture of egg, flour, and milk and then fried

frog   a small animal with a smooth, wet skin. Frogs live near water and jump.

from   out of

front   the side that people usually see or come to first   *front door*

frost   ice that looks like powder and covers things when the weather is very cold

froth   a lot of small bubbles on the top of a liquid

frown   to have lines on your forehead because you are angry or worried

froze, frozen   see **freeze**

fruit   the seed of a plant and the soft or juicy part round it

fry   to cook in hot fat in a pan on top of a stove   *He fried the eggs.*

frying-pan   a large, shallow pan

fudge   a kind of soft, very sweet toffee

fuel   anything that is burnt to make heat   *Coal is a fuel.*

full   with no more room

fund   money that will be used for something special   *We must raise funds for the school trip.*

funeral   the time when a dead person's body is buried or burnt

fungus   a kind of plant that is not green and grows in damp places. Mushrooms and toadstools are both **fungi.**

toadstools

mushrooms

fungi

funnel   **1** a chimney on a ship or railway engine
2 a tube with one very wide end to help you pour things into bottles
Pour the oil through a funnel.

funny   **1** amusing   *a very funny joke*
2 strange   *a funny smell*

fur   the soft hair that covers some animals

furious   very angry

furniture   things such as beds and tables that you need inside a house and can move about

furrow   the straight, narrow hollow made in the ground by a plough

furry   covered in fur

further   to a greater distance   *I swam further than you.*

fuse   **1** a piece of cord used for setting off an explosion
2 a small piece of wire that will melt to stop too much electricity going through. Most plugs have fuses in them.

fuss   to worry and bother too much about something that is not important.

future   the time that will come

G g

gabble   to talk so quickly that it is difficult for other people to understand what you are saying

gadget   a small, useful tool   *A penknife is a useful gadget.*

gain   to get something that you did not have before

galaxy   a very large group of stars that belong together, such as the Milky Way

gale   a very strong wind

galleon   a Spanish ship with sails, used long ago

galleon

gallery 1 a building or long room where paintings are shown *an art gallery*
2 the upstairs seats in a theatre or church

galley 1 a large boat used long ago that needed a lot of men to row it
2 the kitchen on a ship

gallon a measure for liquid *eight pints = one gallon*

gallop to move like a horse moving very quickly

gamble to try to win money by playing a game that needs luck

game something that you play at that has rules. Football and draughts are games.

gander a male goose

gang a group of people who do things together

gangster someone who belongs to a gang that robs and kills people

gangway 1 the plank or set of steps that people walk up to get on to a boat
2 the path between rows of seats in a large building, such as in a cinema

gaol (*say* jail)
prison

gape 1 to have your mouth wide open with surprise *He gaped when he saw his best friend on television.*
2 to be wide open *The workmen left a gaping hole in the road.*

garage 1 the building where a car or bus is kept
2 a place that sells petrol and mends cars

garden a piece of ground where flowers, fruit, or vegetables are grown

gargle to wash your throat by moving liquid around inside it then spitting it out

garter a band of elastic put round a sock to keep it up

gas 1 anything that is like air. Some gases have strong smells.
2 a gas that is burnt to make heat

gash a deep cut

gasp to breathe in noisily and quickly because you are surprised or ill *gasping for breath*

gate a kind of door in a wall or fence round a piece of land

gather 1 to bring together *The children gathered in front of the teacher*
2 to pick *Let's gather blackberries.*

gave see **give**

gay 1 cheerful *a gay tune*
2 brightly coloured *gay curtains*

gaze to look at something for a long time

gear 1 the things needed for a job or sport *camping gear*
2 part of a bicycle or car. Gears help to control the speed of the wheels so that it is easier to go up and down hills.

geese more than one **goose**

gem a valuable or beautiful stone

general 1 belonging to most people or things *The general weather forecast gives an idea of the weather for the whole country.*
2 an important officer in the army *A general is in charge of many soldiers.*

generous always ready to give or share what you have

gentle quiet and kind

gentleman a polite name for a man *Ladies and gentlemen . . .*

genuine real *Is that diamond genuine?*

geography finding out about different parts of the world

geranium a plant with red, pink, or white flowers that is often grown in a pot

gerbil (*begins with the sound* j—)
a small, pale brown animal with long
back legs and very soft fur. Gerbils dig
holes in sand and are often kept as
pets.

gerbil

germ something that is alive but too
small to see and that makes people ill

get **1** to become *My cat is getting old.*
2 to take, buy, or be given something
*I got a new bike yesterday. I'm
getting one for my birthday.*

ghost the shape of a dead person that
people think they have seen moving as
if he were alive

giant one of the very big people in fairy
stories

giddy dizzy

gift a present *a birthday gift*

gigantic (*say* jy-gantic) very big

giggle to keep laughing in a silly way
because you cannot stop yourself

gill the part on each side of a fish that it
breathes through

ginger a powder that gives a strong, hot
taste to sweet things

gingerbread sticky cake or thick
biscuit that tastes of ginger

gipsy one of a group of people with dark
hair and skin, who do not live in houses
but travel from place to place in
caravans. Gipsies are also called
travellers.

giraffe

giraffe a very tall African animal with a
very long neck

girl a female child or teenager

give to let someone have something
*Dad gave me this yesterday. She
was given first prize. I'm giving you a
second chance.*

glacier a river of ice that moves very
slowly down a mountain

glad happy

glance to look at something quickly

glare **1** to look angrily at someone
2 a very strong light *The glare of the
sun hurt my eyes.*

glass **1** something hard that you can
see through. Glass is used for making
windows.
2 a kind of cup that is made of glass
and has no handle

glasses a pair of glass lenses held in front of the eyes by a frame that fits over the nose and ears. People wear glasses to help them to see better.

glen a narrow valley in Scotland and Ireland

glide to move very smoothly *gliding on skates*

glider a kind of aeroplane without an engine

glider

glimmer a very weak light *There was a glimmer of light at the end of the tunnel.*

glimpse to see something for only a few seconds *She glimpsed the school from the window of the train.*

glint to shine with a bright light that comes and goes. *Gold glints.*

glisten to shine like something with drops of water on it

glitter to shine with a bright light that keeps coming and going *glittering jewels*

globe a ball with the map of the whole world on it

gloomy 1 dark *a gloomy room*
2 sad *a gloomy face*

glory 1 great fame
2 great beauty

glossy smooth and shiny

glove a covering for the hand with separate parts for the thumb and each finger

glow to shine with the warm light a fire has

glue a thick liquid for sticking things together

glum not pleased or happy *He looked glum.*

glutton someone who eats too much

gnarled (*say* narled) twisted like the trunk of an old tree

gnat (*say* nat) a thin fly that sucks blood

gnaw (*say* naw) to keep biting something hard like a bone

gnome (*say* nome) a kind of ugly fairy

go to move in any direction *His car goes very fast. She's gone out to play. They went on holiday yesterday. When are you going?*

goal 1 the two posts the ball must go between to score a point in games like football
2 a point scored in football, netball, and other games

goat an animal kept for its meat and milk. Goats often have a strong smell.

gobble to eat very quickly and greedily

goblin a kind of bad, ugly fairy

goes see **go**

go-kart a kind of small, simple racing car

go-karts

gold a valuable, shiny, yellow metal

golden coloured like gold

goldfish a small orange fish often kept as a pet

golf a game played by hitting small, white balls with sticks called clubs, over a large area of ground

gone see **go**

good **1** what people like and praise *good work*
2 kind and true *a good friend*
3 well behaved *a good boy*

goodbye the word you say when you are leaving someone

goods things that can be bought and sold

goose a large bird that is kept for its meat and eggs *two geese*

geese

gooseberry a green berry that grows on a bush with thorns and can be cooked and eaten

gorgeous **1** very attractive
2 with bright colours

gorilla an African animal like a very large monkey with long arms and no tail

gorse a prickly bush with small yellow flowers

gosling a young goose

gossip **1** to talk a lot in a friendly way to someone
2 to talk a lot about other people

got see **get**

govern to be in charge of a place

government the group of people who are in charge of what happens in a country

grab to take hold of something suddenly

grace **1** beautiful movements
The girl danced with grace.
2 a short prayer before or after a meal

gradual happening a little at a time

grain seed that grows in plants like corn and is used for making food

gram a tiny measure for weight
1000 gram = 1 kilogram

grand large, important, or wonderful

grandchild the child of a son or daughter. **Granddaughters** and **grandsons** are grandchildren.

grandfather the father of a father or mother

grandmother the mother of a father or mother

granite a very hard rock

grant to agree to give someone what they have asked for
The fairy granted three wishes.

grape a small, soft green or purple fruit that grows in bunches

grapefruit a fruit that looks like a big orange, but is yellow

graph a diagram that helps you to see how numbers or amounts of things are different from each other

grasp to get hold of something and hold it tightly

grass a green plant with flat, narrow leaves that can be eaten by cattle and other animals

grasshopper

grasshopper   an insect that makes a shrill sound by rubbing one leg against a wing and can jump a long way

grate   **1** a container made of metal bars. Grates hold the coal or wood in a fire.
2 to rub something against a rough surface so that it falls into tiny pieces   *Grate the cheese.*
3 to make the kind of noise the nail on your finger makes if you rub it against a blackboard   *a grating noise*

grateful   wanting to thank someone for what they have done   *He was grateful for her help.*

grave   **1** the hole in which a dead person is buried
2 very serious

gravel   a mixture of sand and tiny stones

gravity   the force that pulls everything towards the earth. If there was no gravity everyone would fall off the earth and float out into space.

gravy   a hot brown liquid poured over meat before it is eaten

graze   **1** to hurt the skin by rubbing hard against something
2 to eat grass as it grows. Cows and sheep graze in fields.

grease   thick, slippery stuff like oil

great   **1** large   *a great amount of money*
2 important   *a great man*
3 very good   *a great idea*

greed   a wish for much more food or money than you really need

greengrocer   someone who keeps a shop that sells fruit and vegetables

greenhouse   a glass building for growing plants in

greet   to welcome someone or say hello

grew   see **grow**

grief   a very sad feeling

grill   to cook food on metal bars put under or over heat

grim   **1** not looking kind, friendly, or pleased   *a grim face*
2 not pleasant   *grim weather*

grin   a smile that shows the teeth

grind   to crush into tiny bits   *The wheat was ground into flour.*

grip   to hold tightly

grit   tiny bits of stone or sand

groan   to make a low sound because you are in pain or trouble

grocer   someone who keeps a shop that sells food, drink, and things like soap powder and matches

groom   **1** someone whose job is to look after horses
2 to make an animal look smart by cleaning and brushing it

groove   a long, narrow hollow. Records have grooves in them.

grope   to try to find something by feeling for it when you cannot see
In the dark she groped for the light switch.

gross   twelve dozen or 144

ground   **1** the earth
2 a piece of land
3 see **grind**

group   a number of people, animals, or things that belong together in some way

grow   **1** to become bigger   *You've grown very quickly.*
2 to plant something in the ground and look after it   *We grew huge leeks last year.*

growl   to make a deep, angry sound. Angry dogs growl.

grown   see **grow**

grub   a tiny creature that will become an insect

grudge   a bad feeling you have against someone, because you think they have harmed you

gruff   with a deep, rough voice

grumble   to keep on saying that you are not pleased about something   *Stop grumbling!*

grunt   to make the sound a pig makes

guard   to keep someone or something safe from other people

guardian   someone who is put in charge of a child whose parents cannot look after him

guess   to say what you think the answer is when you do not really know

guest   someone who is invited

guide   **1** someone or something that shows people which way to go
2 *guide dog* a dog trained to help a blind person

Guide   a girl who is a member of the Girl Guides Association

guilt   a feeling you have when you know you have done something wrong

guilty   full of guilt

guinea pig   a furry animal that has no tail and is kept as a pet

guitar   a musical instrument with strings across it that you play with your fingers

guitars

gulf   sea that fills a very large bend in the land

gulp   to swallow very quickly

gum   **1** the hard pink part of the mouth that holds the teeth
2 a sweet that you chew   *chewing-gum*

gunpowder   a black powder that explodes

gurgle   to make the noise water makes as it goes down the plug-hole in a bath

gush   to move like water rushing out of a tap

gust   a sudden rush of wind or air   *A gust of wind blew the bike over.*

gutter a long, narrow hollow at the side of a street or along the edge of a roof. Gutters take away rain water.

H h ──────────

habit anything that you do without thinking, because you have done it so often *Smoking cigarettes is a bad habit.*

had see **have**

haddock a sea fish that can be eaten

haggard looking ill and very tired *a haggard face*

hail small pieces of ice that fall from the sky like rain

hair a soft covering that grows on the heads and bodies of people and animals

hairdresser someone whose job is to cut people's hair, wash it, or arrange it in a special way

half one of the two equal parts something can be divided into. It can also be written as ½. *Two halves make a whole.*

hall **1** the part inside a house near the front door
2 a very big room *a school hall*
3 a large, important building or house *the Town Hall*

hallo, hello the word you say when you meet someone

Hallowe'en the 31st October when some people think that magic things happen

halt to stop *The train halted at the red light.*

halter a rope or strap put round an animal's head or neck so that it can be controlled

halve to divide into two equal parts

halves more than one **half**

hammer a heavy tool used for hitting nails

hammock a bed that is a piece of cloth hung from something by cords joined to each corner

hammock

hamper **1** a big basket with a lid *a picnic hamper*
2 to make it difficult for someone to do something *The puppy hampered the packing as it kept jumping into the suitcase.*

hamster a small brown animal that has smooth fur and is kept as a pet

hand the part joined to the lower end of the arm

handcuffs a pair of metal rings used for locking someone's wrists together

handicap anything that makes it more difficult for you to do something *The heavy rain was a handicap to the runners.*

handkerchief a square of material used for blowing the nose

handle **1** a part put on something so that you can get hold of it
2 to touch, feel, hold, or use something with your hands   *Handle the kittens carefully.*

handsome attractive. Men and boys can be handsome.

hang to fix the top part of something to a hook or nail   *I hung up my coat and went in.*

hangar a big shed for keeping an aeroplane in

hanger something used for hanging up things

happen **1** to take place   *This must not happen again.*
2 to do something by chance   *I just happened to see it.*

happiness the feeling you have when you are very pleased or enjoying yourself

happy full of happiness

harbour a place where boats can stay safely in the water when they are not out at sea

hard **1** not soft   *hard ground*
2 difficult   *hard sums*
3 severe   *a hard punishment*

hardly only just   *hardly able to walk*

hardware **1** tools, nails, wire and other things made of metal
2 the machinery of a computer

hare an animal like a big rabbit that can move very quickly

harm to hurt or spoil someone or something

harness the set of straps put over a horse's head and round its neck so that it can be controlled

harp a musical instrument. It has a large frame with strings stretched across it that are played with the fingers.

harsh not kind or gentle   *a harsh voice*

harvest the time when farmers gather in the fruit, corn, or vegetables they have grown

has see have

haste hurry   *He forgot all his books in his haste.*

hatch to break out of an egg. Baby birds, insects, fish, and snakes hatch.

hatchet a light tool for chopping

hate to have a very strong feeling against someone or something you do not like

haughty too proud of yourself

haul to pull with all your strength

haunted often visited by ghosts   *a haunted house*

have **1** to own   *She has a new car.   We haven't got a car.*
2 to contain   *The jar used to have sweets in it.*
3 to enjoy or suffer   *We're having a good time.   He's had an accident.*

harp

hawk a bird that hunts and eats smaller animals

hawk

hay dry grass used to feed animals

haze damp or hot air that it is difficult to see through

hazel **1** a small nut tree
2 the light brown colour of a hazel nut

head **1** the part of a person or animal that contains the brain, eyes, and mouth
2 the person in charge

headache a pain in the head that goes on hurting

headmaster a man in charge of all the teachers and pupils in a school

headmistress a woman in charge of all the teachers and pupils in a school

heal **1** to make well again *The cream healed his sore leg.*
2 to become well again *The cut healed quickly.*

health **1** how someone is feeling, either well or ill
2 good health

healthy **1** not ill or injured in any way
2 good for people's health *healthy air*

heap an untidy pile

hear to take in sounds through the ears *I heard you shout so I came.*

heart **1** the part of the body that makes the blood go round inside
2 the curved shape of a heart. Red hearts are printed on some playing-cards.

hearth (*say* harth)
the part of the floor where the fire is

heat **1** the hot feeling that comes from the sun or a fire *The heat made them sleepy.*
2 to make hot *Heat up the soup.*

heath wild, flat land with small bushes, but no trees

heather a low bush with small purple, pink, or white flowers. Heather grows on heaths and moors.

heave to lift or pull something heavy

heaven **1** God's home
2 a very happy place

heavy weighing a lot. It is difficult to lift and carry heavy things.

hedge a kind of wall made by bushes growing close together

hedgehog a small animal covered in stiff hairs like sharp needles

hedgehog

heel the back part of the foot

height **1** how high something is
2 a high place *on the mountain heights*

heir someone who will be given money, property, or a title when their owner dies

heiress a girl or woman who will be given money, property, or a title when their owner dies

helicopter a kind of small aeroplane that can rise straight up into the air. It has large blades that spin round on its roof.

helicopter

helm the handle or wheel that is used to steer a ship

helmet a strong covering that protects the head

help to do something useful for someone else

helpless not able to look after yourself. Babies are completely helpless.

helter-skelter a tall slide at a fair. You go round and round as you slide down it.

hem the edge of a piece of cloth, that is folded under and sewn down

herb a plant used in cooking to give the food a better flavour

herd a number of cattle that feed together

here in or to this place *Come here!*

hermit someone who lives alone and keeps away from everyone else

hero a boy or man who has done something very brave

heroine a girl or woman who has done something very brave

herring a sea fish that can be eaten

herself **1** she and no one else **2** *by herself* on her own

hesitate to wait a little before you do or say something, because you are not sure about it

hibernate to sleep for a long time during the cold weather. Bats, tortoises, and hedgehogs all hibernate.

hiccup to make a sudden, sharp sound. People hiccup when they have eaten or drunk very quickly or laughed a lot.

hide **1** to get into a place where you cannot be seen *I'm hiding over here. I hid behind the tree last time.* **2** to put into a secret place *The gold was hidden in a cave.*

hiding-place a place where someone or something is hidden

helter skelter

70

high **1** going a long way up *a high mountain*
2 a long way up *It flew high into the air.*

highwayman a man on a horse, who stopped people on the roads and robbed them. Dick Turpin was a famous highwayman.

hijack to take control of an aeroplane while it is flying and make it go where you want it to go

hill ground that is higher than the ground around it

himself **1** he and no one else
2 *by himself* on his own

hinder to get in someone's way so that it is difficult for them to do something *The crowds hindered him from getting a close look at the royal family.*

Hindu someone who believes in Hinduism

Hinduism a religion found mostly in India

hinge a metal fastener that joins a door to a wall and lets the door swing backwards and forwards

hinge

hint **1** a useful idea
2 to give someone information without telling them exactly what you mean

hip **1** the bony part of the body that sticks out at the side between the waist and thigh
2 a red berry on the wild rose

hippopotamuses

hippopotamus a very large, heavy, African animal that lives near water. It has a very thick skin.

hire to pay to get the use of something *You can hire skates at the ice rink.*

hiss to make the long sss sound that snakes make

history finding out about things that happened in the past

hive a kind of box for keeping bees in

hoard a secret store of money or other things

hoarse sounding rough and deep. People with sore throats have hoarse voices.

hobble to walk with difficulty because there is something wrong with your leg or foot

hobby something interesting that people like doing in their spare time *Gardening, stamp-collecting, and chess are all hobbies.*

hoe a tool for getting rid of weeds

hold **1** to have something in your hands *I held up the picture I had done.*
2 to have room inside for something *This bag will hold three books.*
3 the place inside a ship where things are kept *Put the cargo in the hold.*

hole a gap or opening made in something

holiday time off from school or work

hollow **1** with an empty space inside *a hollow Easter egg*
2 a kind of hole *Rabbits live in a hollow under the tree.*

holly a tree that has shiny, prickly leaves and red berries in the winter

holly

holster a case for putting a gun in. Holsters are worn on straps or belts.

holy special because it belongs to God

home the place where you live

honest not stealing, cheating, or telling lies *an honest man*

honey sweet, sticky food made by bees

honour great respect

hood a covering of soft material for the head and neck

hoof the hard part round a horse's foot

hoof

hook a piece of bent metal for hanging things on or catching hold of something

hoop a big wooden or metal ring used in games

hoot to make the sound made by an owl or the horn in a car

hope to want something that you think is likely to happen

hopeless **1** very bad at doing something *He was hopeless at games.*
2 without hope *It was hopeless looking for the ball in the long grass.*

hopscotch a game where you hop and throw or kick a stone into squares drawn on the ground

horizon the line where the sky and the land or sea seem to meet

horizontal **1** flat and level
2 *a horizontal line* a straight line across something

horn **1** a kind of pointed bone that grows on the heads of some animals. Bulls and rams have horns.
2 a brass musical instrument that you blow into

horrible **1** nasty *a horrible sight*
2 frightening *a horrible film*

horrid nasty *a horrid dream*

horror very great fear

horse

horse an animal with hooves that is used for riding and pulling carts

horse-chestnut the big tree that conkers grow on

horseshoe a flat piece of metal fixed underneath a horse's hoof

hose-pipe a long plastic or rubber tube that water can go through

hospital a place where people who are ill or hurt are looked after

hostage someone that you hold as a prisoner or threaten with death until you get what you want

hostile being an enemy and acting in a threatening way

hotel a building where people pay to have meals and stay for the night

hound a dog used for hunting

hour sixty minutes

house a building where people live together

household all the people who live together in the same house

hover **1** to stay in one place in the air *The helicopter hovered overhead.* **2** to wait near someone or something and have nothing to do *She hovered about outside the house waiting for her friend.*

hovercraft a machine that is like both an aeroplane and a boat. It travels quickly just above the surface of land or water.

hovercraft

how in what way *How did you know?*

howl to give a long, loud cry like an animal in pain

hub the part at the centre of a wheel, where the spokes meet

huddle to keep close to others in a group because you are cold or frightened

huge very big

hum **1** to sing a tune with your lips closed **2** to make the sound a bee makes

human any man, woman, or child

humble not proud *a humble person*

humorous amusing

humour a sense of humour is when you are able to see the funny side of things

hump one of the big lumps on a camel's back

hung see **hang**

hunger the need for food

hungry feeling hunger

hull the main part of a boat or ship

hunt **1** to go after a wild animal because you want to kill it **2** to look carefully for something *He hunted everywhere for the ring.*

hurl to throw something as far as you can

hurrah, hurray a word that you shout when you are very glad about something

hurricane a storm with a very strong wind

hurry **1** to move quickly *She hurried away to catch her bus.* **2** to try to do something quickly because there is not enough time *He hurried to finish as the bell had gone.*

hurt to make a person or animal feel pain

hurtle to move very quickly *The rocket hurtled through space.*

husband a man married to someone

hustle **1** to hurry
2 to make someone hurry *The teacher hustled the class into the hall.*

hutch a kind of box for keeping a rabbit in

hyacinth a flower that grows from a bulb and has a very sweet smell

hymn a song that praises God

hyphen a mark like this - used in writing to join parts of words together, such as pocket-money

I i

ice **1** water that has frozen hard
2 to put icing on cakes

iceberg a large piece of ice floating in the sea

iceberg

ice-cream a sweet frozen food that tastes of cream

icicle a thin, pointed piece of ice hanging down

icing a sweet, sticky mixture spread over the tops of cakes to decorate them. Some icing goes very hard when it is dry.

idea **1** something you have thought of yourself
2 a plan

ideal just what you want *ideal weather for sailing*

identical exactly the same *identical twins*

idiot a very stupid person

idle doing nothing *idle hands*

idol something people worship and treat as if it were God

igloo a round house made of blocks of hard snow

ignition-key the key used to start the engine of a car

ignorant knowing nothing or only a little *an ignorant fool*

ignore to take no notice of someone

ill not well

illness something that makes people ill. Measles, chicken-pox, and colds are illnesses.

ill-treat to treat badly *It is cruel to ill-treat an animal.*

illuminations a lot of bright, coloured lights used to decorate streets, buildings, or parks

illustration a picture in a book

imaginary not real

imagination the ability to make pictures in your mind of things and people you cannot see

imagine to make a picture in your mind of someone or something you cannot see

imitate to copy a person or animal

imitation a copy that is not as valuable as the real thing

immediately straight away

immense very big

impatient not patient *The impatient man would not wait in the queue.*

impertinent rude, cheeky *an impertinent child*

implore to beg someone to do something for you *He implored his dad to buy the bike.*

important **1** powerful and worth respect *a very important person* **2** worth looking at or thinking about seriously *an important notice*

impossible not possible *It is impossible to jump 10 metres.*

impress to make people think you are very good at something *She impressed her friends with her magic tricks.*

impression a vague idea or feeling *I get the impression he is lazy.*

impressive so wonderful that you will always remember it

imprison to put someone in prison

improve **1** to become better *Her cold is improving.* **2** to make something better *He improved his handwriting.*

incense something that gives a sweet smell when it is burnt

inch a measure for length

include to make something part of a group of other things

incorrect not correct

increase **1** to make bigger *He increased the boy's pocket-money.* **2** to become bigger *The bubble increased in size and then burst.*

indeed really *very wet indeed*

index a list at the back of a book. It tells you what things are in the book and where to find them.

indignant angry because something unfair has been done or said *indignant at getting the blame*

indoors inside a building

industry **1** hard work **2** work done in factories

infant a young child

infectious likely to spread to others *an infectious illness*

inform to tell someone something *She informed the police that her bag had been stolen.*

information words that tell people about something

infuriate to make very angry *The mother was infuriated by the child.*

ingenious clever at thinking of new ways of doing or making things

inhabit to live in a place

initial the first letter of a name *William Brown's initials are W.B.*

injection a prick in the skin made by a hollow needle filled with medicine so that the medicine goes into the body. Injections can make people better or stop them getting illnesses.

injure to harm

injury harm done to part of the body

ink a coloured liquid used for writing with a pen

inland in a part of the country that is not near the sea

inn a kind of hotel in stories

innings a turn at batting in cricket

innocent not guilty, not doing anything wrong

input the information that is put into the memory of a computer

inquiry **1** a question **2** a search to find out all about something

inquisitive full of a wish to know about something. Inquisitive people often want to know about things that they have no right to know about.

insect a tiny creature with six legs. Flies, ants, butterflies, and bees are all insects.

mosquito

butterfly

bee

fly

ant

cockroach   insects

inside **1** in something
2 the part nearest the middle

insist to be very firm in asking, saying, or doing something *He insists on staying up late.*

insolent very rude *insolent behaviour*

inspect to look carefully at people or things

inspector **1** an important policeman
2 someone whose job is to check that things are done properly *ticket inspector*

instalment **1** a part of a story that is told in parts *a serial told in instalments*
2 an amount of money people pay every week or every month in order to buy something

instantly at once

instead in place of something else *They made tea instead of coffee.*

instinct something that makes animals do things they have not learnt to do – they can just do it *Spiders spin webs by instinct.*

instructions words that tell people what to do

instructor a kind of teacher *swimming instructor*

instrument **1** a tool or something else used for doing a job
2 something used for making musical sounds *A drum is a musical instrument.*

insult to hurt someone's feelings by being rude

intelligent able to learn and understand things easily

intend to mean to do something *Do you intend to stay?*

intense very great *intense heat*

interest to make someone want to find out more, look, or listen *A book about animals should interest most children.*

interfere **1** to get in the way
2 to take part in something that has nothing to do with you

international belonging to more than one country *an international competition*

interrupt to stop someone from carrying on with what they are saying or doing

interval the time between parts of a play or film   *Buy an ice-cream in the interval.*

interview to ask someone questions to find out what they think about something or what they are like

introduce to make someone known to other people   *She introduced the new girl to the class.*

invade to go into another country to fight against the people there

invalid someone who is weak because they are ill or injured

invent to be the first person to think of a plan for a new machine or a better way of doing something

investigate to try to find out as much as you can about something

invisible not able to be seen   *invisible ink*

invitation words that ask you politely to come   *a party invitation*

invite to ask someone politely to come or do something

iris 1 the coloured part of the eye
2 a plant with leaves shaped like swords and yellow, white, blue, or purple flowers

irises

iron 1 a strong, heavy metal
2 a flat piece of metal with a handle. It is heated and used for making clothes smooth and flat.

ironmonger someone who keeps a shop that sells tools, nails, and other metal things

irritable easily annoyed   *The child was tired and irritable.*

irritate to keep annoying someone   *The buzzing fly irritated the horse.*

Islam a kind of religion. People who believe in Islam call God Allah.

island, isle a piece of land with water all around it

italic 1 a kind of writing
2 a kind of printing *like this*

itch a feeling in your skin that makes you want to scratch yourself

item any one thing in a list or group of things   *The first item on the shopping list is cheese.*

itself 1 it and nothing else   *The cat yawned and stretched itself.*
2 *by itself* on its own   *The robot can move by itself.*

ivory 1 something that comes from the tusks of elephants. It is pale cream, hard, and very valuable.
2 the pale cream colour of ivory

ivy a climbing plant with shiny dark green leaves

J j

jab 1 to push roughly at something with your finger or the end of a stick   *He jabbed the boy in the back to get his attention.*
2 to hit something suddenly with the pointed part of a sharp tool   *He jabbed his fork into the sausage.*

jackdaw

jackdaw a black bird. Jackdaws sometimes steal bright things and hide them.

jacket a kind of short coat

jagged with sharp parts along the edge

jam **1** fruit boiled with sugar until it is thick *raspberry jam*
2 a lot of people or cars crowded together so that it is difficult to move *a traffic jam*
3 to become fixed and difficult to move *The door has jammed and I can't open it.*

jar a container like the glass ones used for jam

jaw **1** the lower part of the face
2 one of the bones that hold the teeth

jealous unhappy because someone else seems to have more or be doing better than you *She was jealous of her sister's new bike.*

jeans strong cotton trousers

jeep a very strong small car

jeep

jeer to make fun of someone because you think you are better than they are *The crowd jeered at the goalkeeper who let in six goals.*

jelly a sweet, shiny, slippery food that looks solid, though it melts in your mouth *orange jelly*

jerk to move suddenly or clumsily

jersey something with sleeves that is knitted in wool and worn on the top half of the body

jet **1** a liquid or gas coming very quickly out of a small opening *They used a jet spray to paint the car.*
2 an aeroplane with an engine that is driven by jets of hot gas

Jew **1** a person descended from the ancient tribes of Israel
2 a person who believes in Judaism

jewel a valuable and beautiful stone

jewellery necklaces, bracelets, rings, and brooches

jigsaw puzzle a set of small pieces of cardboard or wood that fit together to make a picture

jingle to make the sound tiny bells make

jockey someone who rides horses in races

jog **1** to run slowly
2 to push against something *He jogged my elbow and I spilt the paint.*

join **1** to put together to make one thing *Join the pieces of the jigsaw puzzle.*
2 to become a member of a group *Join the Chess Club.*

joiner someone whose job is to make furniture and other things out of wood

joint **1** the place where two parts fit together. The ankle is the joint between the foot and the leg.
2 a large piece of meat

joke something said or done to make people laugh

jolly happy and cheerful

jolt to shake suddenly *The passengers were jolted on the rough road.*

jotter a book where you can write things down quickly

journey the travelling people do to get from one place to another place

joy great happiness

Judaism the religion of the Jewish people

judge 1 to decide whether something is good or bad, right or wrong, fair or unfair
2 someone who judges *The judge announced the results.*

juggler someone who entertains people by doing difficult throwing, catching, and balancing tricks

juggler

juice the liquid in fruit and vegetables

jumble a lot of different things all mixed up *a jumble sale*

jump to move up suddenly from the ground into the air

jumper a jersey

junction a place where roads or railway lines meet

jungle a forest in a very hot, damp country

junior younger

junk 1 things that people do not want any more
2 a Chinese sailing boat

junk 2

just 1 fair to everyone *a just king*
2 exactly *It's just what I wanted.*
3 only *Just one more cake, please.*

K k

kaleidoscope a thick tube you look through to see coloured patterns. The pattern changes when you turn the end of the tube.

kangaroo an Australian animal that jumps. Female kangaroos have pouches in which they carry their babies.

keel a long piece of wood or metal along the bottom of a boat

keen very interested in something *keen on pop music*

keep 1 to have something as your own and not get rid of it *He kept the money he found.*
2 to make something stay as it is *Try to keep your clothes clean.*
3 to look after something *She keeps rabbits.*

kennel   a little hut for keeping a dog in

kept   see **keep**

kerb   the blocks of stone along the edge of the pavement

kernel   the part in the middle of a nut

kettle   a metal container in which water is boiled. It has a lid, handle, and spout.

key   **1** a piece of metal shaped so that it fits into a lock
2 a small lever pressed with the finger. Pianos and typewriters have keys.

keyboard   the set of keys on a piano, a typewriter, or a computer

kid   a very young goat

kidnap   to take someone away and keep them prisoner until you get what you want

kill   to make someone or something die

kilogram   a measure for weight
a kilogram of apples

kilometre   a measure for length
1 kilometre = 1,000 metres

kilt   a kind of pleated skirt worn by some Scotsmen

kind   **1** ready to help and love other people
2 a sort   *a special kind of paint*

king   a man who has been crowned as ruler of a country

kingdom   a land that is ruled by a king or queen

kingfisher   a brightly coloured bird that lives near water and catches fish

kiosk   **1** a telephone box
2 a small stall that sells newspapers, sweets, and tobacco

kipper   a dried fish that is ready to be cooked and eaten. Kippers have a strong taste.

kiss   to touch someone with your lips because you are fond of them

kitchen   the room where food is cooked

kite   a light frame covered in cloth or paper and flown in the wind at the end of a long piece of string

kite

kitten   a very young cat

knee   the bony part in the middle of the leg where it bends

kneel   to get down on your knees
They knelt down and prayed.

knew   see **know**

knickers   pants worn by women and girls

knife   a tool with a long, sharp edge for cutting things   *two knives*

knight   **1** a man who has been given the title, Sir   *Sir Francis Drake was a knight.*
2 a man in armour who rode into battle on a horse

knit   to use wool and a pair of long needles to make clothes

knives   more than one **knife**

knob   the round handle on a door or drawer

knock   **1** to hit something hard
2 to hit something by accident
He knocked himself on the head.

knot   the twisted part where pieces of string, rope, cotton, or ribbon have been tied together

know 1 to have something in your mind that you have found out *I knew all about it yesterday.*
2 to have met someone before *I haven't known her long.*

knowledge things that are known and understood

known see know

knuckle one of the places where the fingers bend

koalas

koala a furry Australian animal that looks like a small bear

Koran the holy book of Islam that is read in all mosques.

L l ————————————

label a piece of card or sticky paper put on something to show what it is, whose it is, or where it is going

laboratory a room or building where scientific work is done

labour hard work

Labrador a kind of large black or light brown dog

lace 1 thin, pretty material with a pattern of holes in it. Lace is often used to decorate things.
2 a piece of thin cord used to tie up a shoe

lack to be without something *The team lacked a goalkeeper.*

ladder two long bars with short bars between them that you can climb up or down

ladle a big, deep spoon used for serving soup

lady 1 a polite name for a woman
2 a title *Lady Jane Grey*

ladybird a red or yellow insect with black spots on it that can fly

lag to be behind because you are moving too slowly *He's lagging behind again.*

laid see lay

lain see lie

lair a wild animal's home

lake a large area of water with land all around it

lamb a young sheep

lame not able to walk properly

lamp something that gives light where you want it

lance a long spear like the ones used by knights long ago

land 1 all the dry parts of the earth's surface
2 to arrive by boat or aeroplane

landing the flat place at the top of the stairs in a building

landlady a woman who lets other people live in her house or flat in return for money

landlord a man who lets other people live in his house or flat in return for money

lane a narrow road

language words spoken or written by people *foreign languages*

lantern

lantern   a container for a light. It is made of metal and glass or something else that the light can shine through.

lap   **1** the part from the waist to the knees of a person sitting down
2 once round a race course
3 to drink with the tongue, like a cat

larch   a kind of tree. Larches have small cones and lose their leaves every winter.

lard   white fat from pigs, used in cooking

larder   a cool cupboard or small room where food is kept

large   big

lark   a small, brown bird that sings

lash   **1** to tie tightly to something
2 to hit hard, usually with a whip

lasso

lasso   (*say* la-soo)
a long rope with a loop at the end, tied so that the loop can get bigger or smaller. Cowboys use lassos for catching cattle.

last   **1** after all the others   *go out last*
2 to go on for some time   *The film lasted one hour.*

latch   a fastener on a gate or door

late   **1** after the expected time
2 near the end of a day, month, or year
3 no longer alive   *the late King*

lather   soap bubbles on the top of water

laugh   to make sounds that show that you are happy or think something is very funny

laughter   the sound of laughing

launch
1 a large boat with an engine
2 to push a boat into the water
They launched the lifeboat to rescue some people.
3 to send a spaceship from earth into space

launderette   a place with washing-machines that people can pay to use

laundry
1 clothes that need to be washed
2 a place where people send dirty clothes and sheets to be washed

lavatory   a toilet

lavender 1

lavender   **1** a bush with pale purple flowers that smell very sweet
2 a pale purple colour

law   a rule or set of rules that everyone in a country must keep

lawn   the part of a garden that is covered with short grass

lay   **1** to put something down
2 *to lay the table* to get the table ready for a meal
3 to make an egg   *The hen laid two eggs today.*
4 see **lie**

layer   something flat that lies over or under another surface   *a layer of icing on the cake*

lazy   not willing to work

lead¹   (*rhymes with* bed)
a soft, grey metal that is very heavy

lead²   (*rhymes with* seed)
1 to go in front of other people to show them where to go or what to do   *He found us and led us to safety.*
2 to be in charge of a group   *You lead this team.*
3 a strap fastened to a dog's collar so that you can control it   *Keep your dog on its lead.*

leader   a person or animal that leads

leaf   one of the flat green parts that grow on trees and other plants

league   a group of teams that play matches against each other

leak   to have a hole or crack that liquid or gas can get through

lean   **1** to bend your body towards something   *I leant forward and looked.*
2 to rest against something   *Lean against me if you are tired.*
3 to make something slope   *Lean the ladder against the wall.*
4 not fat   *lean meat*

leant   (*say* lent)
see **lean**

leap   to jump   *I leapt up as if I'd been stung.*

leapt   (*say* lept)
see **leap**

leap year   a year with an extra day in it, the 29th February. A leap year comes once every four years.

learn   **1** to find out about something
2 to find out how to do something   *He learnt to swim last year.*

leash   a dog's lead

least   **1** less than all the others
the least expensive bike
2 the smallest amount   *The least you can do is say you are sorry.*

leather   a strong material made from the skins of animals   *leather shoes*

leave   **1** to go from a person or place
2 to let something stay where it is
I've left my book at home.

leaves   more than one **leaf**

led   see **lead**²

ledge   a narrow shelf like the one that sticks out under a window

leek   a long, white vegetable with green leaves that tastes like an onion

leeks

left   **1** on the side opposite the right. Most people hold a fork in their left hand and a knife in their right hand.
2 see **leave**

left-handed   using the left hand to write and do other important things, because you find it easier than using the right hand

legend a story that was first told long ago by people who thought it was true. Most legends are not true.

leisure (*rhymes with* treasure) time when you can do what you want to do, because you do not have to work

lemon **1** a pale yellow fruit with a sour taste
2 the pale yellow colour of lemons

lemonade a drink made from lemons, sugar, and water

lend to let someone have something of yours for a short time
I lent you my bike yesterday.

length **1** how long something is
2 a piece of rope or cloth

lengthen **1** to make longer *You can lengthen a rubber band by stretching it.*
2 to get longer *The days lengthen in March.*

lens a curved piece of glass or plastic that makes light go where it is needed. Spectacles, cameras, and telescopes have lenses.

lent see **lend**

leopard a big wild cat found in Africa and Asia. It has yellow fur with black spots on it.

leopard

leotard (*say* lee-a-tard)
a piece of clothing worn by acrobats and dancers

less **1** not as much
2 take away. Six less four is two, $6 - 4 = 2$.

lessen **1** to make less *Take out some shopping and it will lessen the weight of the bag.*
2 to become less

lesson **1** the time when someone is teaching you
2 something that you have to learn *Road safety is an important lesson for everyone.*

letter **1** one of the signs used for writing words, such as a, b, or c
2 a written message sent to another person

lettuce a vegetable with green leaves that are eaten in salads

level **1** flat and smooth *level ground*
2 equal *Your scores are level.*

lever a bar that is pulled down to lift something heavy or make a machine work

liable **1** likely to do or get something
2 responsible for something

liar someone who tells lies

library a building or room where a lot of books are kept for people to use

licence a printed paper that says that you can do, own, or use something *a dog licence*

lick to move the tongue over something

lie **1** to rest with the body flat as it is in bed *I lay down and went to sleep. The cat has lain here all night. He has been lying here.*
2 to say something that is not true *You lied to me yesterday. He was lying.*
3 something you say that is not true *He tells lies.*

life the time between birth and death *Do cats have nine lives?*

lifeboat

lifeboat   a boat that goes out to sea in bad weather to save people's lives

lift   **1** to move upwards   *Lift out the shopping from the trolley.*
2 to pick up something   *Can you lift this heavy box?*
3 a machine for taking people or things up and down inside a building
4 a ride in someone's car or lorry

light   **1** the power that makes things able to be seen. Light comes from the sun, the stars, flames, and lamps.
2 to start something burning   *I struck a match and lit the fire.*
3 pale   *light blue*
4 weighing little   *as light as a feather*

lighten   **1** to make lighter   *We need to lighten the ship's cargo.*
2 to get lighter   *The sky lightened as the sun rose.*

lighthouse   a tower with a bright light that warns ships of rocks or other dangers

lighthouse

lightning   the bright light that flashes in the sky during a thunderstorm

like   **1** to think someone or something is pleasant
2 nearly the same as another person or thing

likely   expected to happen or to be true   *He is the likely winner of the race as he has trained hard.*

lilac   **1** a tree with a lot of white or pale purple flowers that smell very sweet
2 a pale purple colour

lily   a beautiful white flower

limb   a leg, arm, or wing

lime   **1** a white powder used in making cement
2 a pale green fruit like a lemon
3 a kind of tree

limit   a line or point that people cannot or should not pass   *a speed limit*

limp   **1** walk with difficulty because there is something wrong with your leg or foot
2 not stiff   *The cardboard box became limp and soggy in the rain.*

line   **1** a long, thin mark like this
————————————
2 a row of people or things
3 the set of metal rails a train moves along

linen   strong cloth used for making sheets and table-cloths

liner   a big ship for taking people on long journeys

linger   to be slow to leave   *After the concert they lingered outside hoping to meet one of the band.*

lining   cloth covering the inside of clothes or curtains

link   **1** to join things together
2 one of the rings in a chain

lino, linoleum   a stiff, shiny covering for the floor

lint   soft material for putting on an injured part of the body

lion   a large, light brown wild cat found in Africa and India

lioness   a female lion

lipstick   something that looks like a crayon and is used for colouring lips

liquid   anything that is like water, oil, or milk

liquorice   a black sweet that you get in sticks and other shapes

list   a group of things or names written down one after the other   *a shopping list*

listen   to pay attention in order to hear something

lit   see **light**

litre   (*rhymes with* Peter) a measure for liquid   *a litre of paint*

lobster

litter   **1** paper, empty packets, bottles, and other rubbish, dropped or left lying about
2 all the young animals born to the same mother at the same time   *The cat had a litter of seven kittens.*

little   **1** not big   *a little boy*
2 not much   *little time*

live¹   (*rhymes with* give)
1 to have your life
2 to have your home in a place

live²   (*rhymes with* dive)
alive   *Careful! This electricity wire is live.*

lively   full of life and energy   *a lively dance, a lively horse*

lives   (*rhymes with* dives)
more than one **life**

lizard   a creature with skin like a snake and four legs

load   **1** something that is carried
The lorry was carrying a heavy load.
2 to put things on to something that will carry them   *Load the suitcases into the car boot.*
3 to put bullets into a gun   *Load the gun.*

loaf   bread in the shape it was baked in
two loaves

loan   anything that is lent to someone

loaves   more than one **loaf**

lobster   a sea creature with a shell, two large claws, eight legs, and a tail

local   belonging to one place   *local radio*

loch   a lake in Scotland

lock   **1** to fasten with a key   *Turn the key to lock the door.*
2 a fastening for a door, gate, or box that is opened with a key   *The key is stuck in the lock.*
3 a piece of hair   *She cut her golden locks.*

locomotive   the engine that pulls a train

locust   an insect that flies about in a large group, destroying plants by eating them

locust

lodge **1** to pay to live in someone else's house
2 a small house near the gates of a large garden that belongs to a much bigger house

lodger someone who pays to live in another person's home

lorry

loft a room in the roof, where things can be kept

loiter to stand about with nothing to do

loll to sit or lie in an untidy, lazy way

lollipop a big sweet on the end of a stick

lonely **1** sad because you are on your own
2 far from others *a lonely house*

long **1** measuring a lot from one end to the other *a long road*
2 taking a lot of time *a long holiday*
3 *to long for* to want something very much

look **1** to use your eyes
2 *to look for* to try to find something
3 to seem *You look sad.*

loom a machine for weaving cloth

loop a ring made in rope, wire, thread, or ribbon

loose (*say* looss)
1 not tight *His baby tooth was loose.*
2 not fixed to anything *The dog is loose – he has shaken off his lead.*

loosen **1** to make looser *He loosened his tie.*
2 to get looser *The opening and closing of the door has loosened the screw.*

loot things that have been stolen *a hoard of loot.*

lord **1** a nobleman
2 a title *Lord Baden-Powell*

lorry a big, open truck for taking heavy things by road

lose (*say* looz)
1 to be without something you once had
2 to be without something, because you cannot find it *I've lost my coat.*
3 to be beaten in a game *We lost last Saturday's match.*

lost see **lose**

lotion a liquid that is put on the skin

loud **1** very easy to hear
2 noisy

loudspeaker **1** a machine that makes sound louder
2 the part of a television, radio, or record-player that the sound comes from

lounge a room with comfortable chairs in it

love to like very much

lovely **1** beautiful *a lovely face*
2 pleasing *a lovely idea*

low not high

loyal always true to your friends

luck the way things happen that have not been planned

lucky having good luck *a lucky charm*

luggage bags, boxes, and suitcases taken by someone on a journey

lukewarm only just warm

lullaby a song that is sung to send a baby to sleep

lumber   **1** rough wood
   2 to move in a clumsy way

lump   **1** a solid thing with no clear shape
   a lump of clay
   2 a swelling

lunch   a meal eaten in the middle of the day

lung   one of the two parts inside the body used for breathing

lurch   to lean suddenly to one side
   The train lurched and the passengers were thrown about.

lurk   to wait where you cannot be seen
   The boy lurked in the bushes hoping to surprise his friends.

luxury   something expensive that you like very much but do not really need

lying   see **lie**

M m ————————————

mac   short for **mackintosh**

machine   something with several parts that work together to do a job
   a washing-machine

machine-gun   a gun that can keep firing very quickly for a long time

machinery   machines

mackintosh   a raincoat

madam   a word sometimes used when speaking politely to a woman, instead of her name

made   see **make**

magazine   a kind of thin book that comes out every week or month with different stories and pictures in it

maggot   a tiny worm that comes from an egg laid by a fly

magic   the power to do wonderful things or clever tricks that people cannot usually do

magician   someone who knows a lot about magic and uses it

magnet   a metal bar that can make pieces of iron or steel come and stick to it

magnet

magnificent   **1** very grand
   a magnificent palace
   2 splendid   *a magnificent present*

magnify   to make something look bigger   *a magnifying glass*

magpie   a black and white bird. Magpies sometimes steal bright things and hide them.

maid   a girl or woman who is a servant

mail   letters, cards, and parcels sent through the post

main   the most important   *a main road*

majesty   a word used when speaking to a king or queen   *Your Majesty*

make   **1** to get something new by putting other things together   *I've made a boat out of paper and wood.*
   2 to cause something to happen
   You made me do this last time.

make-up   cream, lipstick, and powder put on the face to make it look different

make-up

male any person or animal that can become a father. Men, boys, stags, and bulls are all males.

mammal any animal that has hair and can feed its babies with its own milk *Whales, lions, and people are all mammals.*

man a fully grown male *two men*

manage **1** to be in charge of a shop or factory *Her job was to manage the factory.*
2 to be able to do something although it is difficult *After a chase they managed to catch the rabbit.*

mane the long hair along a horse's back or on a lion's head and neck

manger a long, narrow container that horses and cattle can eat from when they are in the stable

mangle to cut up or crush something roughly

manner the way something happens or is done

manners your behaviour towards other people *She taught her children to have good manners.*

manor a big, important house in the country

mansion a big, important house

mantelpiece the shelf above a fireplace

manufacture to make large numbers of the same thing

many a large number of people or things

map a diagram that shows part of the world and where different places are

marble **1** a small, glass ball used in some games
2 a kind of smooth stone used for building or making statues

march to walk like soldiers on parade

mare a female horse

margarine a food that looks and tastes like butter, but is not made from milk

margin the empty space between the edge of a page and the writing or pictures

marigold a bright orange or yellow flower grown in gardens

marigold

mark **1** a stain, spot, or line that spoils something *dirty marks*
2 a sign or number put on a piece of work to show how good it is

market a group of stalls selling food and other things. Markets are usually held in the open air.

marmalade jam made from oranges or lemons

maroon **1** a very dark red colour
2 to leave someone in a wild and lonely place without any way of escaping from it *After the shipwreck he was marooned on an island.*

marriage a wedding

marry to become someone's husband or wife

marsh a piece of very wet ground

marvellous wonderful *a marvellous story*

marzipan a sweet food made from almonds

mash to crush something to make it soft and get rid of the lumps *mashed potato*

masks

mask a covering worn on the face to protect or hide it

mass **1** a large number or amount *masses of flowers*
2 A Roman Catholic church service

massive very big

mast a tall pole that holds up a ship's sails, a flag, or an aerial

master a man who is in charge

match **1** a small, thin stick that gives a flame when rubbed on something rough
2 a game played between two sides
3 to be the same as another thing or like it in some way *In some card games you have to find the matching pictures.*

material **1** anything used for making something else *Cement and bricks are building materials.*
2 wool, cotton, or anything else that is woven and used for making clothes or covers

mathematics, maths finding out about numbers, measurement, and shapes

matter **1** to be important *Does it matter if I arrive late?*
2 something you need to think about or do *a serious matter*
3 *What's the matter?* What is wrong?

mattress the thick, soft part of a bed

may **1** can *May I go out to play?*
2 will perhaps *It may rain later. It might rain later.*

mayor the person in charge of the council in a town or city

maze a set of lines or paths that twist and turn so much that it is very easy to lose the way

maze

meadow a field covered with grass

meal the food eaten at breakfast, lunch, dinner, tea, or supper

mean **1** not generous *She's mean – she never shares her sweets.*
2 to plan in your mind *I meant to tell him, but I forgot.*
3 to have a meaning *This dictionary tells you what words mean.*

meaning what someone wants to say with the words they are using
The angry farmer's meaning was clear: we must keep off his land.

meant (*rhymes with* tent) see **mean**

melon

meanwhile during the time something else is happening *You set the table. Meanwhile I'll prepare the lunch.*

measles an illness that makes red spots come on the skin

measure 1 to find out how big something is
2 a unit used for measuring. Kilograms, grams, pounds, and ounces are all measures for weight.

measurement how much something measures

meat the flesh of animals used as food

mechanical worked by or like machinery *a mechanical digger*

medal a piece of metal in the shape of a coin, star, or cross given to someone very brave or very good at something *a gold medal*

medallist someone who has won a medal

meddle to take part in something that has nothing to do with you *Don't meddle in their quarrel.*

medicine liquid or tablets that a sick person has to swallow in order to get better again

medium of middle size

meek gentle and not proud

meet 1 to come together
2 to come face to face with another person *I met her in town yesterday.*

meeting a group of people who have come together to talk about something or to listen to someone

melon a large, juicy fruit with a yellow or green skin

melt to change into a liquid when heated. Ice melts.

member someone who belongs to a group

memory 1 the ability to remember
2 anything that is remembered *The old man had happy memories of when he was a boy.*
3 the part of a computer that stores information

men more than one **man**

menagerie a kind of small zoo

mend to make a damaged thing as useful as it was before

mention to speak of something or someone when you are talking about other things *He was talking about the zoo and she mentioned that she liked animals.*

menu a list of the different kinds of food you can choose for your meal

mercy being kind to someone instead of punishing them *Show mercy to the prisoners.*

meringue (*say* me-<u>rang</u>)
a crisp cake made from the whites of eggs mixed with sugar and baked

mermaid a creature in stories, that looks like a woman but has a fish's tail instead of legs

merry happy and gay

mess things that are untidy, dirty, or mixed up

message   words that you send to someone to tell him something when you cannot speak to him yourself

messenger   someone who takes a message to someone else

met   see **meet**

metal   something hard that melts when it is very hot. Gold, silver, iron, and tin are all kinds of metal.

microscope

meteor   a small piece of rock or metal that moves through space and burns up when it gets near the earth

meteorite   a lump of rock or metal that has fallen through space and landed on the earth

meter   a machine that measures how much of something has been used   *gas meters*

method   the way you choose to do something   *His method of adding numbers was very strange.*

metre   a measure for length   *1,000 metres = 1 kilometre*

metric system   a way of measuring things. The metric system uses metres for measuring length, kilograms for measuring weight and litres for measuring liquids.

mew, miaow   (*say* mee-<u>ow</u>) to make the cry a cat makes

mice   more than one **mouse**

microchip   one of the tiny pieces used to make a computer

microcomputer   the kind of computer people might use in their homes or on their desks at work

microphone   a machine that changes sound into electricity so that it can be sent along wires to loudspeakers, telephones, or aerials

microscope   an instrument that makes it possible to see very tiny things by making them look much bigger

microwave oven   an electronic oven that cooks food very quickly

midday   twelve o'clock in the day

middle   the part of something that is the same distance from all its sides or edges or from both its ends

midnight   twelve o'clock at night

might   see **may**

mild   gentle

mile   a measure for length

milk   a white liquid that mothers and some female animals feed their babies with. People can drink cows' milk.

mill   **1** a place with machinery for making corn into flour
2 a kind of factory   *A paper mill makes paper from wood.*

millionaire   someone who owns a million pounds

mime   to tell someone something by using actions not words

mimic   to copy someone's voice in order to make fun of them

mince   meat cut into very small pieces

mincemeat   a sweet mixture of chopped fruit and other things, cooked inside pastry at Christmas

mind **1** the power to think, feel, and understand
2 to look after   *I'll mind the baby.*
3 *Mind out!* Be careful!
4 to be worried or upset by something   *Do you mind missing the party?*

mine **1** a place where people work to dig coal, metal, jewels, or salt out of the ground
2 a bomb hidden in the ground or the sea to blow up things that come close to it
3 belonging to me   *That's mine.*

miner someone who works down a mine

mineral **1** any useful or valuable rock people get out of the ground
2 a cold drink with a lot of tiny bubbles in it

mingle to mix

miniature tiny, but just like something much bigger

minister someone who serves God by being in charge of a church

minnow a tiny fish found in rivers, streams, lakes, and ponds

minstrel a man who sang or played music to entertain people long ago

mint **1** a green plant used in cooking to give food a better flavour
2 a sweet that tastes of mint   *a peppermint.*
3 a place where coins are made

minus take away. Six minus two is four, $6 - 2 = 4$.

minute[1] (*say* <u>min</u>-it) sixty seconds

minute[2] (*say* my-<u>newt</u>) very tiny

miracle something wonderful that has happened, although it did not seem possible

mirage a trick of the light that makes people see things that are not really there, such as pools of water in deserts

mirror a piece of glass, in which you can see yourself

misbehave to be naughty

mischief silly or bad behaviour that gets you into trouble

mischievous likely to do silly or naughty things   *The mischievous puppy pulled the washing from the line.*

miser someone who has a lot of money, but tries to spend as little as possible so that they can keep it

miserable very unhappy

misery suffering   *great misery*

misfortune something unlucky that happens

miss **1** to fail to hit, catch, see, hear, or find something
2 to be sad because someone is no longer with you

mission an important job that someone is sent away to do

mist damp air that it is difficult to see through

mistake something you have done or thought that is wrong   *spelling mistakes*

mistletoe a plant which grows on other trees. It is used to decorate houses at Christmas.

mistletoe

misunderstand to get the wrong idea about something *You misunderstood what I said.*

mitten a kind of glove with two parts, one for the thumb and one for all the fingers

mix to stir or shake different things together to make one thing

mixture something made of different things mixed together

moan **1** to make a soft sound that shows you are in pain or trouble *The boy moaned as they lifted him into the ambulance.*
2 to grumble *The class moaned about missing the swimming lesson.*

moat a ditch dug round a castle and usually filled with water

mock **1** to make fun of someone
2 not real *a mock battle*

model **1** a small copy of something *He made a model aeroplane.*
2 someone whose job is to wear new clothes to show people what they look like *The model wore the latest fashions.*

modern of the kind that is usual now *a modern house*

moist damp

mole

mole a small, grey, furry animal that digs holes under the ground

moment a very small amount of time

monarch a ruler who is a king, queen, emperor, or empress

monastery a house where monks live and work

money the coins and pieces of paper used when people buy and sell things

mongrel a dog that is a mixture of different kinds of dog

monitor a boy or girl with a special job to do at school

monk one of a group of men who live together and obey rules because of the religion they believe in

monkey an animal with hands, feet it can use like hands, long arms, and a tail

monster a large, frightening animal in stories

month a measure for time. There are twelve months in a year.

monument a statue or building made so that people will remember someone or something

mood the way you feel *in a good mood*

moon the planet that goes round the earth and shines in the sky at night. Sometimes it looks completely round and sometimes like part of a circle.

moor **1** an area of land that has bushes but no trees, because it is too windy
2 to tie up a boat so that it will not float away

more **1** a larger number or amount
2 again *I'll tell you once more.*

morning the time from the beginning of the day until the middle of the day

mortar a mixture of sand, cement, and water, used in building to stick bricks together

mosaic

mosaic   a picture made from coloured pieces of paper, glass, stone, or wood

moss   a plant that grows in damp places and has no flower

mosque   a building where Muslims worship

most   **1** more than any other
2 very   *She was most kind.*

moth   an insect with large, coloured wings. Moths usually fly around at night.

moths

mother   a female parent

motor   the part inside a car or machine that makes it move

motorbike   a kind of bicycle with an engine

mould   (*rhymes with* old)
1 a kind of fungus. It is the furry stuff that sometimes grows on food that has gone bad.
2 a container for making things like jelly or plaster set in the shape that is wanted

mound   a pile of earth

mount   to get on to a horse or bicycle so that you can ride it

mountain   a very high hill

mouse   a very small animal with a long tail and a pointed nose   *three blind mice*

moustache   hair that grows above a man's top lip

mouth   the part of the face that opens for eating and speaking

move   **1** to take from one place to another
2 to go from one place to another.

movement   moving   *a sudden movement*

mow   to cut grass

much   a lot of something

mud   wet soil

muddle   to mix things up and make a mess of something

muesli   a food made of cereals, nuts, and dried fruit

mule   an animal that is half horse and half donkey

multiply   to make something a number of times bigger. Two multiplied by four is eight: $2 \times 4 = 8$.

mumble   to speak in a way that is not clear so that it is difficult to hear your words

mumps   an illness that makes the sides of the face swell

munch   to chew noisily

murder   to kill someone on purpose

murmur   to speak in a very soft, low voice

muscle   one of the parts inside the body that become tight or loose in order to make the body move

museum a place where a lot of interesting things are kept for people to go and see

mushroom a kind of fungus that people can eat

music the sounds made by someone singing or playing a musical instrument

musical 1 having to do with music *musical instruments*
2 good at music

Muslim someone who believes in the religion of Islam

mussels

mussel a small sea creature that lives inside a pair of black shells

must have to *I must go now.*

mustard 1 a yellow powder or liquid used to give food a strong flavour
2 *mustard and cress* small green plants eaten in salads

mutiny an attack made by soldiers or sailors against the officers in charge of them

mutter to murmur or grumble *'Why does it always have to be me?' he muttered to himself.*

mutton meat from a sheep

muzzle 1 an animal's nose and mouth
2 a cover put over an animal's nose and mouth so that it cannot bite

myself 1 I and no one else
2 *by myself* on my own

mysterious strange and puzzling

mystery something strange and puzzling that has happened

N n

nag to keep telling someone that you are not pleased and that they ought to behave differently *She nagged him to tidy his room.*

nail 1 the hard·part that covers the end of each finger and toe
2 a small piece of metal with a sharp point, used for fastening pieces of wood together

naked (*say* nay-kid) without any clothes or covering

name what you call someone or something

nanny 1 someone who looks after young children
2 a grandmother

nanny-goat a female goat

nappy a piece of cloth put round a baby's bottom

narrow not wide

nasty 1 not pleasant *a nasty day*
2 very dirty *a nasty mess*
3 not kind *a nasty person*

nation a country and the people who live in it

national belonging to one country

native someone born in the place that you are thinking of *a native of Scotland*

natural 1 made by nature, not by people or machines
2 normal *It is natural for birds to fly.*

nature 1 plants, animals, the sea, and everything else in the world that was not made by people
2 what a person or animal is really like *My dog has a very gentle nature.*

naughty   badly behaved

navigate   to make sure that a ship, aeroplane, or car is going in the right direction

navy   **1** a group of ships and the people trained to use them for fighting
2 dark blue

near   not far away

nearly   not quite   *nearly 3 o'clock, nearly £100, nearly there*

neat   tidy

necessary   needed very much
It is necessary to water plants in hot weather.

neck   the part of the body that joins the head to the shoulders

necklace   beads, jewels, or a chain worn round the neck

nectar   a sweet liquid inside flowers. Bees collect nectar to make honey.

need   **1** to be without something that you ought to have
2 to have to do something   *I need to go to the dentist.*

netball

needle   **1** a very thin, pointed piece of metal. Needles used for sewing have holes in them.
2 one of a pair of rods used for knitting
3 a very thin, pointed leaf. Pine trees have needles.

neglect   to leave something alone and not look after it   *He neglected the garden and it was full of weeds.*

neigh   to make the noise a horse makes

neighbour   someone who lives next door or near to you

neither   not either   *Neither of the twins has a bike.*

nephew   the son of a brother or sister

nerve   **1** one of the small parts inside the body that carry messages to and from the brain, so that the body can feel and move
2 brave or calm behaviour when there is danger   *Don't lose your nerve.*

nervous   **1** afraid and excited because of something you have to do   *She was nervous before the exam.*
2 easily frightened   *a nervous animal*

nest   a cosy place made by birds, mice, and some other animals for their babies

nestle   to curl up comfortably   *He nestled down in bed.*

netball   a ball game played outside between two teams of girls. The ball has to be thrown into a net on a tall post.

nettle   a plant with its stem and leaves covered in hairs that sting

never   not ever

new   **1** just bought or made   *a new bike*
2 different   *my new school*

news   words that tell you about something that has just happened

newspaper   large sheets of paper folded together, with the news printed on them. Most newspapers come out every day.

newt

newt a small creature that lives near water and has four legs and a long tail

next the nearest

nib the pointed metal part at the end of the kind of pen that needs ink

nibble to eat something by biting off a little at a time. Rabbits nibble carrots.

nice pleasant

nickname a name you call someone instead of his real name. William Cody's nickname was Buffalo Bill.

niece the daughter of a brother or sister

night the time when it is dark

nightingale a small, brown bird that sings at night

nightmare a frightening dream

nimble able to move quickly and easily *Her nimble fingers sewed the tiny stitches.*

nip to bite someone or squeeze their skin between the thumb and finger

nitwit someone who is very silly

noble brave and generous

nobleman a man who is a duke or lord

nobody no person

noise sound that is loud and often not pleasant

none not any or not one

nonsense something that does not mean anything

noon twelve o'clock in the day

no one no person

noose a loop made in a piece of rope so that when the rope is pulled the loop gets smaller

normal usual or ordinary *The normal time for school to start is 9 o'clock.*

north the direction to your left when you face east

northern from the north or in the north

nose the part of the face that is used for breathing and smelling

nostril one of the two holes at the end of the nose for taking in air

notch a mark like a V, cut into something

note **1** a short letter
2 one sound in music *Play a note on the piano.*

nothing not anything

notice **1** to see something and think about it *She noticed the milk bottles were still on the doorstep.*
2 something fixed to a wall or a piece of board, for you to read *Please read the notice-board.*

nought the sign for nothing, 0

noun any word that tells you what someone or something is called. *Air, Ann, speed, England,* and *chair* are all nouns.

nourish to feed someone well

novelty something new or unusual

now at this time

nowhere not anywhere

nozzle the part at the end of a piece of pipe where a spray of liquid or powder comes out

nude without any clothes

O

nudge to push someone with your elbow to make them notice something

nugget a lump of gold

nuisance someone or something that causes trouble *It's a nuisance that we missed the bus.*

numb not able to feel anything

number the word or sign that tells you how many. 1, 2, and 3 are numbers.

numerous many

nun one of a group of women who live together and obey rules because of the religion they believe in

nurse someone whose job is to look after people who are ill or hurt

nursery a place where very young children go to play and be looked after

nut **1** a kind of fruit that you chew after you have taken off its hard shell *walnut, peanut*
2 a short piece of metal that is screwed on to the end of a bolt to make it firmer

nutmeg a hard seed that is made into a powder and used in cooking to give food a better flavour

nylon a very strong thin material for making clothes and other things

obedient willing to do what you are told to do *His dog is always very obedient.*

obey to do what you are told to do

object¹ (*say* <u>ob</u>-ject) anything that can be seen or touched

object² (*say* ob-<u>ject</u>) to say that you do not like or agree with something

oblong the shape of a door or this page

observe **1** to watch carefully *We observed the robin building her nest.*
2 to say something that you have noticed

obstacle something that is in the way

obstinate not willing to change your ideas even though they might be wrong

obstruct to be in the way so that something cannot get past *A fallen tree was obstructing the road.*

obtain to get

obvious very easy to see or understand *The answer to the problem was obvious.*

occasion the time when something happens *a special occasion*

occasionally sometimes

occupation any job or hobby

O o

oak a large tree with seeds called acorns

oar a long pole with a flat part at one end, used for rowing a boat

oasis a place with water and trees in a desert

oath a serious promise made to God

oats a plant grown by farmers. Its seed is used for feeding animals and for making food such as porridge.

oasis

occupy **1** to live in something
2 to keep someone busy and interested *Keeping young children occupied is a hard job.*

occur **1** to happen
2 to come into your mind *An idea occurred to me.*

ocean a big sea

o'clock by the clock *one o'clock*

octopus a sea creature with eight arms

octopus

odd **1** strange *an odd person*
2 not even *Five is an odd number.*
3 not alike *odd shoes*

odour a smell

off **1** away *They ran off.*
2 not on *Turn the tap off.*

offend to hurt someone's feelings

offensive nasty and very annoying *an offensive smell*

offer **1** to hold out something so that another person can take it if they want it
2 to say that you are willing to do something *He offered to tidy the classroom.*

office a room with desks and telephones, where people work

officer someone in the army, navy, or air force, who is in charge of others

often many times

ogre (*say* o-ger)
a giant who eats people

oil a thick, slippery liquid. Oil is put in machines to make them work better and is burnt to make heat. Another kind of oil is used in cooking.

ointment a cream for putting on sore skin or cuts

old **1** born or made a long time ago *He's an old man. He's nearly ninety.*
2 not new *It's an old car. We've had it ten years.*

old-fashioned of the kind that was usual a long time ago *old-fashioned clothes*

omelette eggs that are mixed together and fried

omit to leave out *She omitted the first story and just read the second one.*

once **1** one time *She only missed school once that term.*
2 at one time *Once dinosaurs roamed the earth.*

onion a round, white vegetable with a very strong flavour

only **1** no more than *only two cakes*
2 one by itself *the only one left*

ooze to come slowly through a hole or small opening. Blood oozes from small cuts. *Toothpaste was oozing through a hole in the tube.*

open **1** not closed
2 to make open

opera a play in which all or most of the words are sung

operation **1** something done by doctors to a sick person's body to make it healthy again
2 the working of a machine

opinion what you think of something

opportunity a good chance to do something

opposite **1** facing *The house on the opposite side of the road is for sale.*
2 something that is as different as possible from another thing. Hot is the opposite of cold.

optician someone who makes or sells spectacles

orange **1** a round, juicy fruit with thick peel and white pips
2 the colour of this fruit

orbit the path in space of something moving round the sun or a planet. The moon is in orbit round the earth.

orchard a place where a lot of fruit trees grow

orchestra a large group of people playing musical instruments together

ordeal a time when you have to put up with great pain or trouble

order **1** to tell someone to do something *The officer ordered the soldiers to march.*
2 to ask for something to be brought to you *He ordered fish and chips in the café.*
3 *in order* properly arranged

ordinary not special in any way

ore a piece of rock with metal in it

organ a large musical instrument like a piano, with pedals and pipes

organize **1** to get people working together to do something
2 to plan and arrange things like parties, concerts, or holidays *She is good at organizing things.*

original **1** made first, before any others
2 new and not copied from anywhere *an original idea*

ornament something put in a place to make it look pretty

orphan a child whose mother and father are dead

ostrich

ostrich a very large bird that cannot fly and has long legs

other not the same as this *The other sweets were better.*

otherwise or else

otter

otter a furry animal that lives near water. Otters have long tails.

ought should *I ought to go now.*

ounce a measure for weight

ourselves **1** we and no one else *We tidied the room ourselves.*
2 *by ourselves* on our own

out **1** not in
2 not burning *The fire has gone out.*

outcast   someone ignored and left by their family and friends

outfit   clothes that are worn together   *a Brownie outfit*

outing   a day or afternoon out somewhere   *an outing to the zoo*

outlaw   someone long ago who had to hide, because, as a punishment they were not protected by the law and anyone could kill them. Robin Hood was a famous outlaw.

outline   a line round the edge of something, that shows its shape

outside   **1** not inside
2 the surface or edges of something

outskirts   the parts on the outside of an area or town

outstanding   unusually good
outstanding work

oval   the shape of an egg

oven   the space inside a stove, where food can be baked or roasted

over   **1** above or covering   *He pulled his hood over his head.*
2 finished   *Playtime is over.*
3 left   *Is there any food over?*
4 more than   *There were over 40,000 at the match.*

overall   including everything

overalls   something worn over other clothes to keep them clean

overboard   over the side of a boat into the water   *Man overboard!*

overflow   to come over the sides of a container, because there is too much in it

overhead   **1** above the head
overhead wires
2 in the sky above   *a plane flying overhead*

overtake   to catch up and pass someone

overturn   to push or knock something over

owe   to have to pay money to someone

owl   a bird with large eyes that hunts smaller animals at night

own   **1** to have something that belongs to you
2 *to own up* to say that you were the one who did something
3 *my own* mine and no one else's
4 *on my own* by myself

ox   a large animal kept for its meat or for pulling carts   *two oxen*

oxygen   the gas in the air that everyone needs to breathe in order to stay alive

oyster   a sea creature that lives inside a pair of shells

P p

pace   **1** one step
2 how quickly something happens or moves

pack   **1** to put things into a box, bag, or suitcase in order to move them or store them
2 a group of dogs or other animals
a pack of wolves
3 a group of Brownies or Cubs
4 a set of cards used in games

package   a parcel

packet   a small parcel

pad   **1** sheets of writing paper joined together along one edge so that you can tear a sheet off when you need it
2 soft material folded up into a kind of cushion to protect something
3 to walk softly

paddle   **1** to walk about in shallow water   *I like paddling.*
2 a thin piece of wood with a flat part at the end, used to make a canoe move

padlock

palm **1** the inside of the hand between the fingers and wrist
2 a tropical tree with large leaves and no branches

pamper to treat a person or animal too well *Granny pampered the children and brought them breakfast in bed.*

pancake flour, milk, and egg mixed together and fried

panda an animal found in China. Giant pandas look like large black and white bears.

panda

padlock a lock joined to something by a metal loop

page **1** one side of a piece of paper that is part of a book
2 a little boy who walks behind the bride at a wedding

paid see **pay**

pail a bucket

pain the feeling you have when part of your body is injured or sick

paint **1** a coloured liquid put on the surface of something to colour it *We bought a tin of paint.*
2 to use paint to colour something *Paint the door blue.*

painting a picture that has been painted

pair two people, animals, or things that belong together *a pair of gloves*

palace a very large house where a king, queen, or some other very important person lives

pale **1** almost white *a pale face*
2 light *a pale blue sky*

palette a piece of board on which artists mix their colours while they are painting

paling a wooden fence

pane a piece of glass in a window

panel a long, flat piece of wood or metal that is part of a door, wall, or piece of furniture

panic sudden fear that cannot be controlled

pansy a small plant with a brightly coloured flower

pant to take the short, quick breaths you take after running a lot

panther an Indian leopard

pantomime a kind of play, usually done at Christmas. It tells a fairy story and has singers and comedians in it.

pantry a small room where food is kept

pants **1** underpants
2 trousers

paper **1** wet rags, straw, or tiny pieces of wood pressed and dried into very thin sheets. Paper is used for making books and wrapping up things.
2 a newspaper

parable a story told by Jesus in order to teach people something

parachute

parachute a large piece of cloth that opens up like an umbrella when a cord is pulled. It is tied to someone's back so that they can jump out of an aeroplane and float safely down to the ground.

parade people marching along, while other people watch them

paraffin a liquid made from oil, that is burnt to make heat

parallel lines straight lines that are always the same distance from each other

paralysed not able to move or feel anything

parcel something wrapped up ready to be carried or posted

pardon to forgive

parent **1** a person who has a child
2 an animal that has young ones

parish an area that has its own church and priest or minister. Some parishes have their own schools.

park **1** a large garden where anyone can walk or play
2 to leave a car somewhere for a time until it is needed again

parliament the group of people that makes the laws of a country

parrots

parrot a brightly coloured bird that can learn to repeat things that are said to it

parsley a green plant used in cooking to give a stronger flavour to food

parsnip a pale yellow vegetable with a sweet taste

part anything that belongs to something bigger *He had a big part in a play.*

particle a very tiny piece *particles of dust*

particular only this one and no other

partner one of a pair of people who dance together or play on the same side in a game

party a group of people enjoying themselves together *a Christmas party*

pass **1** to go by *On my way to school I pass the shop.*
2 to give someone something they want, but cannot reach themselves *Please pass the salt.*
3 to be successful in a test *She's passed her driving test.*

passage a corridor

passenger anyone travelling in a bus, train, ship, or aeroplane, except the driver and crew

Passover a holy time for Jews

passport special papers printed by the government that a person has to have with them in order to go to another country

past **1** the time that has gone *In the past people used horses to travel.*
2 up to and further than something *Go past the school.*

pasta (*say* pass-ta)
a food made from flour and water. Spaghetti is one kind of pasta, but there are many other shapes and sizes.

paste a wet mixture used for sticking paper to things

pastime something you do or play in your free time *Her favourite pastime is watching television.*

pastry a mixture of flour, fat, and water rolled flat and baked

pasture land covered in grass that cattle, sheep, or horses can eat

patch **1** a small piece of material put over something to mend it or protect it
2 a small piece of ground *They have a vegetable patch.*

path a very narrow way that you can go along to get somewhere

patience the ability to be patient

patient **1** someone who is ill and being looked after by a doctor *The patient lay in the hospital bed.*
2 able to bear pain or able to wait for a long time without getting angry *They sat in the queue patiently.*

patrol a group of soldiers or policemen who move around a place to guard it

patter to make the light, tapping sound rain makes against a window

pattern **1** a set of lines and shapes drawn on something to make it look pretty
2 anything that people copy in order to make something *a dress pattern*

pause to stop for a very short time

pavement the part at each side of a street for people to walk along safely

pavilion the building where people playing games such as cricket can leave their things or wait for their turn

paw an animal's foot

pay to give money in return for something *I paid for the sweets last time.*

pea a tiny, round, green vegetable that grows inside a pod

peace **1** a time free from war
2 a time of quiet and rest *We enjoy the peace and quiet when the baby is asleep.*

peaceful quiet

peach a round, soft, juicy fruit with a large stone and a thin, yellow skin

peacock

peacock a large bird with very long, brightly coloured tail feathers that it can spread out like a fan

peak **1** the top of a mountain
2 the part of a cap that sticks out in front

peal to make a loud, ringing sound

peanut a tiny, round nut that grows in a pod in the ground

pear a juicy fruit that is narrow where the stalk is

pearl a small, shiny, white ball found inside the shells of some oysters. Pearls are used for making valuable jewellery.

pearl necklace

peat soil that is formed from decaying plants. It can be dug up in solid pieces and burnt instead of coal.

pebble a small, round stone

peck to use the beak to pick up food or push at something

peculiar strange *a peculiar taste*

pedal a part that is pressed with the foot to make something work. A bicycle has two pedals.

pedestrian someone who is walking

peel the skin on some fruit and vegetables

peep to look quickly or secretly

peer to get very close to something to look at it *They peered at the writing and tried to read it.*

pelican a sea bird with a very large beak

pellet a tiny ball of wet paper, metal, food, or medicine

pelt **1** an animal's hair and skin
2 to throw a lot of things at someone *They pelted the boys with snowballs.*

penalty a kind of punishment *The referee gave a penalty against us to the other side.*

pence more than one **penny**

pencil a thin wooden stick with another coloured stick inside it, used for writing and drawing

pendant something hung round the neck on a long chain or string

pendulum a rod with a weight hanging from its end so that it swings backwards and forwards. Some clocks are worked by pendulums.

penetrate to make or find a way through something *The cold wind penetrated even his winter coat.*

penguin a sea bird that cannot fly and uses its short, stiff wings for swimming

penguins

penknife a small knife that folds up so that you can carry it with you safely

penny a coin *100 pence = £1 She counted out six pennies.*

people men, women, and children

pepper a powder used to give food a stronger flavour. It can make you sneeze.

peppermint   a sweet with a strong mint flavour

perch   **1** anything that a bird rests on when it is not flying
2 to sit on the edge of something, like a bird on a branch

percussion instrument   any musical instrument that is banged, hit, or shaken. Drums, cymbals, and tambourines are percussion instruments

perfect   so good that it cannot be made any better

perform   to do something in front of an audience

performance   something done in front of an audience   *The last performance of the play was on Friday night.*

perfume   a liquid with a very sweet smell

perhaps   possibly   *Perhaps it will rain tomorrow.*

peril   danger   *the perils of the sea*

perimeter   the distance round the edge of something

perish   **1** to die   *The sailors perished in the storm.*
2 to become dry and wrinkled and no longer any use. Rubber perishes.

permanent   able to last for a very long time without changing   *This ink is permanent – it won't wash out.*

permission   words that say something is allowed   *They got permission to go to the cinema.*

permit   to allow   *Weather permitting, we shall go for a walk this afternoon.*

persist   to carry on doing something no matter what happens   *The child persisted in crying for more even though the sweet packet was empty.*

person   a man, woman, or child

persuade   to get someone to agree to something   *She persuaded her mum to buy her the coat.*

pest   any person, animal, or plant that causes a lot of trouble   *Flies are a pest.*

pester   to keep worrying someone by asking questions   *He pestered his dad about getting a new bike.*

petal   one of the separate, coloured parts of a flower. Daisies have a lot of white petals.

petrol   a liquid made from oil. Petrol is put in the engines of things such as cars and aeroplanes to make them go.

petticoat   a piece of clothing worn underneath dresses and skirts

pew   one of the long wooden seats in a church

pew

phone   short for **telephone**

photo, photograph   a picture taken with a camera and printed on paper

phrase   a group of words, such as *at the seaside*

physical   having to do with the body   *physical education*

piano   a large musical instrument with white and black keys that are pressed with the fingers

pick   1 to choose
2 to take something up from where it is   *Pick up that sweet paper.*
3 to take flowers or fruit from plants and trees
4 a pickaxe

pickaxe   a heavy tool with a long handle, for breaking up very hard ground

pickles   vegetables stored in vinegar

picnic   a meal eaten in the open air away from home

picture   a painting, drawing, or photograph

pie   meat or fruit covered with pastry and baked

piece   a part of something   *a piece of cake*

pier   something long that is built out into the sea for people to walk on. Some piers have shops on them and places where people can enjoy themselves.

pierce   to make a hole through something   *The straw pierced the bottle top.*

pigeon   a bird that can be taught to fly home from far away

pile   a number of things put on top of one another

pilgrim   someone who makes a journey to a holy place

pill   a small, round tablet

pillar   a wooden or stone post that helps to hold up a building

pillion   the seat on a motorbike behind the rider's seat

pillow   the cushion that you rest your head on in bed

pilot   1 someone who steers an aeroplane
2 someone who steers a ship in narrow, difficult places

pimple   a small, round swelling on the skin

pincers   a tool for holding something tightly

pinch   1 to squeeze skin between the thumb and finger in order to hurt someone
2 to take without asking   *Who's pinched my pencil?*

pine   1 to get ill because you miss someone very much   *The dog pined for his master who was on holiday.*
2 a tree with cones for its seeds and clusters of leaves that look like green needles

pineapple

pineapple   a large fruit that grows in hot countries. It has stiff, pointed leaves and a thick skin covered in lumps.

pint   a measure for liquid   *a pint of beer*

pioneer   1 one of the first people to go and live in a new country
2 someone who is the first to do something

pipe   1 a tube for taking gas or water somewhere
2 a tube with a small bowl at one end, used for smoking tobacco

pirate   someone on a ship, who attacks and robs other ships

pistol   a small gun

pitch **1** ground marked out for cricket, football, or another game
2 a black, sticky liquid made from tar
3 to put up a tent
4 to throw *He pitched the ball high over our heads.*

pitchfork a tool like a very large fork, for lifting hay

pity the feeling you have when you are sorry that someone is in pain or trouble

pivot a point that things swing from, spin round, or balance on. Wheels and see-saws have pivots.

pivot

pixie, pixy a kind of fairy *Do you believe in pixies and goblins?*

pizza
a flat piece of dough covered with tomatoes, cheese, and other things, and baked

placard a notice

place **1** any space where something belongs
2 To put something in a particular place

plague a dangerous illness that spreads very quickly

plaice a sea fish that can be eaten

plain **1** not decorated *a plain sponge cake*
2 not pretty
3 easy to understand *The meaning is plain.*
4 a large area of flat ground *On the plain you could see for miles.*

plait (*say* plat)
1 to twist together pieces of wool, cord, thread, straw, or hair by crossing them over and under each other
2 a long piece of plaited hair

plan **1** to decide what is going to be done
2 a map of a building or town

plane **1** short for **aeroplane**
2 a tool for making wood smooth
3 a tall tree with large leaves

planet any of the worlds in space that move round the sun. The earth is a planet.

plank a long, flat piece of wood

plant anything that grows out of the ground. Trees, bushes, and flowers are all plants.

plaster **1** a sticky strip of special material for covering cuts
2 a soft mixture that goes hard when it dries. Plaster is used in building, mending broken bones, and making models.

plastic something light and strong that is made in factories and used for making all kinds of things *plastic bowls, plastic bags*

plasticine something like clay only soft and coloured, which you can make into different shapes with your hands

plate a flat dish for eating from

platform **1** a small stage *The teacher stood on the platform to speak to the whole school.*
2 the place in a station where people wait beside the railway lines for a train

play **1** to be in a game
2 to make music with a musical instrument
3 a story that is acted *He went to the theatre to see a play.*

playground a place out of doors where children can play

playing-card   one of a set of cards used in some games

playtime   the time at school when children can go out to play

plead   to beg for something that you want very much   *She pleaded with her parents to buy a dog.*

pleasant   pleasing   *a pleasant holiday*

please   **1** to make someone happy
2 the polite word you use when you are asking for something   *Please may I have another cake?*

pleasure   the feeling people have when they are pleased

pleat   **1** a flat fold made in the material of a dress, skirt, or kilt
2 *pleated*   with pleats

plenty   **1** a lot of something   *There was plenty of food for everyone.*
2 more than enough   *No more crisps, you've had plenty.*

pliers   a tool for holding something tightly or for bending or breaking wire

a pair of pliers

plimsoll   a light, canvas shoe with a rubber sole

plod   to walk slowly and heavily

plot   **1** to plan secretly   *They plotted how to trick him.*
2 a small piece of ground   *They cleared a plot to grow vegetables.*

plough

plough   (*rhymes with* cow) a machine used on farms for digging and turning over the soil

pluck   **1** to pull a feather, flower, or fruit from the place where it is growing
2 to pull at something and let it go quickly. People play guitars by plucking the strings.

plucky   brave   *The plucky boy dived in to save the drowning cat.*

plug   **1** a part joined to a lamp or machine by wire. It fits into a place in a wall where electricity can come into it.
2 a round piece of rubber or metal that fits into a hole. It stops water running out of a bath or sink.

plum   a juicy fruit with a stone in it

plumber   someone who puts in and mends taps and water pipes

plume   a large feather

plump   fat

plunge   **1** to jump suddenly into water
2 to put something suddenly into water   *He plunged the burning cloth into a bowl of water.*

plural   any word when it is written differently to show that it means more than one. *Cakes, children, ladies, mice,* and *monkeys* are all plurals.

plus   add. Three plus three is six, $3 + 3 = 6$.

plywood   a kind of wood made from thin sheets of wood glued together

pneumonia   (*say* new-monia) a serious illness that makes it painful to breathe

poach   **1** to cook an egg in boiling water or steam without its shell
2 to hunt animals that are on someone else's land

polar bear

pocket   a part like a small bag, sewn into some clothes

pod   a long seed case that grows on some plants. Peas grow inside pods.

poem   a piece of writing with a special rhythm. Poems are usually written out in short lines.

poet   someone who writes poetry

poetry   poems

point   **1** the sharp end of things such as pins and pencils
2 a mark scored in a game
3 to show where something is by holding out your finger towards it
4 to aim a weapon

pointed   with a point at the end

poison   any liquid, powder, or plant that will kill or harm you if you swallow it

poisonous   likely to harm you because it contains poison   *poisonous berries*

poke   to push hard with the end of your finger or a stick

poker   a metal rod for poking a fire

polar bear   a very large, white bear that lives in the Arctic

pole   **1** a long, round stick of wood or metal
2 either of the two ends of a magnet
3 *North pole* the place that is the furthest north in the world
4 *South pole* the place that is the furthest south in the world

police   the people whose job is to catch criminals and make sure that the law is kept. There are thousands of **policemen** and **policewomen** in Britain.

polish   to rub the surface of something to make it shine

polite   having good manners

pollen   the yellow powder inside a flower. Pollen helps to make seeds.

pollution   dirty and unhealthy air or water. Smoke and waste from factories cause pollution.

pond   a very small lake

ponder   to think about something carefully

pony   a small horse

poodle   a kind of dog with curly hair often cut very short on some parts of its body

pool **1** a small area of water
  2 a game like snooker

poor **1** having very little money *a poor family*
  2 bad
  poor work, poor light

poplar a tall, straight tree

poppies

poppy a bright red flower often found growing near corn

popular liked by a lot of people

population the number of people who live in a place

porch a small place with a roof, in front of the door of a building

pork meat from a pig

porpoise a sea animal like a small whale

porpoise

porridge a hot food made from oats boiled in water or milk, eaten at breakfast

port a large place where ships can stay safely in the water when they are not at sea

portable able to be carried about *a portable television*

porter someone whose job is to carry other people's luggage at places like hotels and railway stations

portion the part or amount given to you
Get a small portion of chips.

portrait a picture of a person

posh very smart

position **1** the place where something is or should be *This is a good position to pitch the tent.*
  2 how the body and its parts are arranged *a sitting position*

positive completely sure *I am positive I gave you the book.*

possess to own *She possessed five pairs of shoes.*

possible able to happen or to be done
It is possible it might snow tonight.

post **1** an upright pole fixed in the ground
  2 to send a letter, parcel, or card

postcard a piece of card that you can write a message on and post. Postcards often have pictures on one side.

postcode a group of letters and numbers that show the district a person lives in, so that the post office can deliver the mail more quickly

poster a large notice for everyone to read

postman someone who collects and delivers letters and parcels

post office a place that sells stamps and deals with letters and parcels

postpone   to put off until later   *They postponed the race until the rain had stopped.*

potato   a vegetable dug out of the ground   *baked potatoes*

potion   a drink with medicine or poison in it

pottery   cups, plates, and other things made out of baked clay

pouch   **1** a small bag
2 a kind of pocket that some animals have in their skin. Hamsters have pouches inside their cheeks.

pouffe   (*rhymes with* roof) a low seat that is like a large, firm cushion

poultry   birds kept for their meat and eggs   *Hens and turkeys are poultry.*

pounce   to attack something by jumping on it suddenly   *The rat pounced on the mouse.*

pound   **1** a measure for weight   *five pounds of potatoes.*
2 a measure for money, also written £   *£1 = 100 pence*
3 to beat very hard with the fists   *He pounded on the door to make them hear.*
4 to crush something by hitting it hard

pour   **1** to make liquid run out of a container
2 *to pour with rain* to rain hard

pout   to stick out your lips when you are not pleased

powder   anything that is very dry and made up of many separate tiny bits, like flour or dust

power   **1** the ability to do something
2 strength

powerful   very strong or important

practical   **1** able to do useful things   *A penknife is a practical gadget.*
2 likely to be useful   *a practical idea*

practice   something you keep doing in order to get better at it   *piano practice*

practise   to do something over and over again in order to get better at doing it   *If you keep practising you will soon improve.*

prairie   a very large area of flat ground covered in grass, in North America

praise   to say that someone or something is very good

pram   a kind of cot on wheels for a baby

pram

prance   to jump about in a very lively way   *a prancing horse*

pray   to talk to God

prayer   talking to God

preach   to speak to other people just as a priest does in church

precious   very valuable   *a precious jewel*

precipice   a very steep part of a mountain or rock

prefer   to like one person or thing more than another person or thing   *She preferred singing to dancing.*

pregnant   expecting a baby

prehistoric   belonging to a time very long ago   *prehistoric animals*

preparations   things that are done to get ready for something   *The preparations for Christmas start in October.*

prepare to get something ready

present¹ (*say* <u>prez</u>-ent)
1 something given to someone *a birthday present*
2 the time now *Our teacher is away at present.*
3 here *All present and correct, sir!*

present² (*say* pri-<u>zent</u>)
to give someone a prize or gift in front of other people

presently soon

preserve **1** to keep safe
2 to do things to food so that it will not go bad

president someone chosen to rule a country that does not have a king or queen

press **1** to push hard on something *Press the doorbell.*
2 to make clothes smooth and flat with an iron

pressure **1** pressing on something *The pressure of the pile of books squashed the box.*
2 how much one thing is pressing on another *Test the air pressure of the car tyre.*

pretend to make it seem that something not true is true *He pretended he was ill.*

pretty pleasant to look at *a pretty girl, a pretty dress*

prevent to stop something from happening *You can prevent pollution.*

previous coming before this one *the previous week*

prey **1** any animal hunted and eaten by another animal
2 *a bird of prey* a bird that hunts and eats other animals

price the amount of money you have to pay for something

priceless very valuable

prick to make a tiny hole in something

prickle a sharp part like a thorn

pride the feeling people have when they are proud

priest **1** someone who serves God by being in charge of a church
2 a man who leads people in their religion

primary school the school you go to from when you are about five years old until you are about twelve

Prime Minister the most important person in the government

primrose a small, pale yellow flower that comes out early in the spring

primroses

prince the son of a king or queen

princess **1** the daughter of a king or queen
2 the wife of a prince

principal most important or chief

principle an important rule

print **1** to write with letters that are not joined together
2 to use a machine that presses words and pictures on to paper. Books, newspapers, and magazines are printed.

prison a place where criminals are kept as a punishment

prisoner **1** someone who has been captured
2 someone in prison

private   **1** not open to everyone
a private road
2 not known by other people
a private thought

prize   something that is won

probable   likely to be true or to happen
What's the most probable result?

problem   something that is difficult to
understand or to answer

proceed   to go on   *The carnival parade
proceeded slowly along the street.*

procession   a group of people moving
along in a long line

prod   to push something with the end of
a finger or stick

produce   **1** to make
2 to bring something out so that it can
be seen

producer   the person in charge of the
acting of a play

profit   the extra money got by selling
something for more than it cost to buy
or make

program   a list of instructions for a
computer

```
1Ø  CLS                          program
2Ø  LET X = 1Ø: Let Y = 1Ø
3Ø  Let A$ = INKEY$
4Ø  IF A$ = "" THEN GOTO 3Ø
5Ø  IF A$ = "A" THEN LET Y = Y-1
6Ø  IF A$ = "Z" THEN LET Y = Y+1
7Ø  IF A$ = "N" THEN LET X = X-1
```

programme   **1** a talk, play, or show on
the radio or television
2 a list for people in an audience telling
them about what they will see or hear

progress   **1** moving forward   *We've
been in the queue for an hour but we're
making slow progress.*
2 getting better   *All the class made
good progress in arithmetic.*

prohibit   to say that people must not do
something   *Smoking Prohibited*

project   **1** finding out as much as you
can about something interesting and
writing about it   *a project on flight*
2 a plan

projector   a machine for showing
films or photographs on a screen

promenade   a kind of road made by the
sea where people can walk

promise   to say that you will certainly
do or not do something   *He's always
promising us things.*

prompt   without delay

prong   one of the thin, pointed parts on
the end of a fork

pronounce   to say a sound or word in a
certain way

proof   something that shows that an
idea is true

prop   **1** a long piece of wood or metal
put underneath something to support it
2 to support one thing by leaning it
against another thing   *The ladder was
propped up against the wall.*

propel   to drive forward

propeller   a set of blades that spin
round. Propellers are fixed to
aeroplanes, helicopters, and ships to
make them move.

propeller

propeller

proper correct *in the proper place*

property things that belong to someone

prophet someone who tells people what is going to happen, although nobody knows

prosecute to make someone go to court so that they can be punished if they have done wrong *Trespassers will be prosecuted*

prosper to become successful or rich

protect to keep safe from danger

protection something that protects

protest to say or show that you think what someone else is saying or doing is wrong

proud 1 full of the idea that you are better or more important than you really are
2 very pleased because you or someone belonging to you has done well *He is proud of his sister.*

prove to show that an idea is true

proverb something often said in order to help people, such as 'A stitch in time saves nine.'

provide to give something that is needed

prowl to move about like an animal looking for something to kill and eat

prune a dried plum

pry to try to find out about something that has nothing to do with you *He liked to pry into other people's business.*

psalm (*say* sarm) one of the hymns in the Bible

public 1 all the people *the general public*
2 open to everyone *Everyone came to the public meeting.*

a Christmas pudding

pudding something sweet and made to be eaten after the main part of a meal *Christmas pudding*

puddle a small pool of dirty water

puff 1 a small amount of breath, wind, or smoke
2 to blow out puffs of smoke or air
3 *puffed* out of breath

puffin a sea bird with a large orange and blue beak

pull to get hold of something and make it come towards you

pulley a wheel with rope round it, used for lifting heavy things *They lifted the car engine using a pulley*

pulley

pullover a jersey or jumper

pulp anything that has been made soft and wet *fruit pulp, paper pulp*

pulpit the high wooden desk in a church, where the priest stands to talk to the people

puppet 1

puppet 2

pulse the throbbing that can be felt at the wrist as the blood is pumped around inside the body

pump 1 a machine that pushes liquid or air through pipes *She filled the car with petrol from the pump.*
2 to push air or liquid into something *Pump up that flat tyre.*

pumpkin a very large, round fruit with a hard yellow skin

punch 1 to hit with the fist
2 a tool for making holes in paper or leather

punctual exactly on time *Please be punctual or the coach will leave without you.*

punctuation marks such as commas and full stops put into a piece of writing to make it easier to read

puncture a hole in a tyre

punish to make someone who has done wrong suffer, so that they will not want to do wrong again *People who break the law are punished and sent to prison.*

punishment something done to punish someone

pupil 1 someone who has a teacher
2 the black spot at the centre of the eye

puppet 1 a kind of doll whose head and limbs can be moved by strings and rods
2 a kind of doll with a body like a glove, so that you can move its head and arms with your fingers

puppy a very young dog

purchase to buy

pure with nothing else mixed with it *pure water*

purpose what someone means to do *He trod on my toe on purpose not by accident.*

purr to make the sound a cat makes when it is very pleased

purse a small bag for holding money

pursue to run after someone and try to catch them *The policeman pursued the thief.*

push to use your hands to move something away from you

put to move something into a place

putty something soft and sticky that sets hard, used for fixing glass into windows

puzzle 1 a game or question that is difficult to work out and makes you think a lot *a crossword puzzle*
2 to make someone think very hard to find the answer *a puzzling question*

pyjamas trousers and a jacket worn in bed

pylon a metal tower that holds up high electric cables

pyramid 1 a large, stone building made by the ancient Egyptians to hold the body of a dead king or queen. Pyramids have sloping sides that meet in a point at the top
2 the shape of a pyramid

python a very large snake

Q q

quack to make the sound a duck makes

quadrilateral a flat shape with four sides and four corners

quail 1 a wild bird that can be eaten 2 to look frightened

quaint unusual but pleasant *a quaint cottage*

quake to shake because you are very frightened *She was quaking with fear*

quality how good or bad something is *You need best quality paper for model-making.*

quantity an amount *She added a small quantity of salt to the dough.*

quarrel to speak angrily to someone or fight with them, because they do not agree with you *He often quarrelled with his brother.*

quarry 1 a place where people cut stone out of the ground so that it can be used for building 2 an animal that is being hunted *In a fox-hunt the fox is the quarry.*

quarter one of the four equal parts something can be divided into. It can also be written as ¼.

quay (*say* key) a place where ships can be loaded and unloaded

queen 1 a woman who has been crowned as ruler of a country 2 a king's wife

queer very strange

quench 1 to put an end to someone's thirst *The tea quenched her thirst.* 2 to use water to put out a fire *The bucket of water quenched the spreading flames.*

query (*say* queery) a question that you ask about something, because you think it might be wrong *She had a query about the plans.*

quest a long search *The knight set off on a quest to find lost treasure.*

question something that you ask when you want to find out or get something

queue (*say* cue) a line of people waiting for something

quick 1 done in less time than usual *a quick snack* 2 fast *Be quick!*

quiet 1 without any noise 2 not loud *a quiet voice*

quill 1 a big feather from a bird's wing or tail 2 a pen made from a feather

quilt a bed cover like an eiderdown. It has lines of stitching across it to keep the filling in place.

quite 1 completely *I'm quite sure.* 2 *quite big* big, but not enormous

quiver 1 to shake because you are very cold or frightened 2 a bag for carrying arrows

quiz a kind of game in which people try to answer a lot of questions in order to show how much they know *two quizzes.*

R r

rabbi a teacher of Judaism

rabbit a furry animal with long ears. Rabbits live in holes they have dug in the ground.

race a competition to find the fastest

rack a set of bars made into a shelf or something else that people can put things on *a luggage rack*

racket 1 a kind of bat with a wooden or metal frame and string stretched across it in a criss-cross pattern *a tennis racket*
2 a lot of loud noise *What a racket all those barking dogs made.*

rackets 1

radiant 1 bright *radiant sunshine*
2 looking very happy *a radiant smile*

radiate to give out heat or light *Warmth radiated from the fire.*

radiator 1 a metal container or a set of pipes that gives out heat in a room
2 the part inside a car for keeping the engine cool

radio a machine that receives sounds sent as electrical waves and changes them into programmes and messages that people can listen to

radish a small, hard, round, red vegetable, eaten raw in salads

radius the distance from the centre of a circle to the edge *two radii*

raffle a kind of sale held to get money for something. People buy tickets with numbers on them and certain numbers win prizes.

raft something flat made of pieces of wood joined together and used instead of a boat

rafter one of the long, sloping pieces of wood that hold up a roof

rage great anger

raid a sudden attack on a place

rail 1 a bar or rod
2 a long metal bar that is part of a railway line

railings a fence made of metal bars

railway the set of metal bars that trains travel on

rain drops of water that fall from the sky

rainbow the curved band of different colours seen in the sky when the sun shines through rain

rainbow

raincoat a coat made of waterproof material for keeping you dry when it rains

raise 1 to lift up or make something higher
2 to gather together the money or people needed for something *We need to raise money for the school trip.*

raisin a dried grape used in cooking

rake a tool used in the garden. It has a long handle and a row of short spikes.

rake

rally   a large number of people who have come together for a big meeting

ram   **1** a male sheep
2 to push one thing very hard into another thing   *She rammed the cork into the bottle.*

raspberries

Ramadan   a holy time for Muslims when they fast during the day

ramble   a long walk in the country

ran   see **run**

ranch   a large American farm with a lot of cattle or horses

random   *at random* without any plan or aim

rang   see **ring**

rank   **1** a title or job that shows how important someone is. The rank of general is higher than the rank of captain.
2 a row of people   *The soldiers stood in neat ranks.*

ransack   to search everywhere for something and leave things looking very untidy

ransom   money paid so that a prisoner can be set free

rap   to knock quickly and loudly   *She rapped on the door and told them to hurry up.*

rapid   very quick

rare   not often found. Pandas are rare animals.

rascal   **1** a naughty child
2 someone who is not honest

rash   **1** done in a rush without any thought about what might happen   *a rash action*
2 red spots or patches that suddenly come on the skin   *a measles rash*

raspberry   a soft, sweet, red berry

rate   how quickly something happens or is done

rather   **1** fairly   *It's rather cold.*
2 more willingly   *I'd rather have a cake.*

rattle   **1** to make quick, hard noises by shaking something
2 a baby's toy that rattles

rave   to talk in a very excited or enthusiastic way   *He raved about his holiday saying it was his best ever.*

raven   a large, black bird

ravenous   very hungry   *She had missed her breakfast and lunch and was ravenous at supper.*

ravine   (*say* ra-<u>veen</u>)
a very deep, narrow space between mountains

raw   not cooked

ray   a thin line of light   *the sun's rays*

razor   a very thin, sharp blade. Men shave their faces with razors.

reach   **1** to stretch out the hand in order to touch something   *He reached for a cake.*
2 to arrive at a place

reaction   an action in reply to something that has happened or has been done   *What was Dad's reaction to the broken window?*

read[1] (*say* reed)
to be able to say and understand words that are written down   *I've read this before.*

read[2] (*say* red)
see **read**[1]

ready   **1** able and willing to do something at once   *Are you ready yet?*
2 fit to be used at once   *Everything is ready.*

real   not a copy   *a real diamond*

realize   to come to understand something clearly   *He realized that the furry lump was in fact a kitten.*

really   truly   *Is it really snowing?*

realm   (*rhymes with* helm)
the land a king or queen rules

reap   to cut down and gather in the corn when it is ready

rear   **1** the back part of something   *Sit at the rear of the bus.*
2 to look after children or young animals until they are big   *She reared the puppies.*
3 to stand on the back legs and lift the front legs into the air, like a dog begging   *The horse reared in fright when it saw the snake.*

reason   anything that explains why something has happened

reasonable   **1** fair   *a reasonable price*
2 sensible   *It is not reasonable to play outside in the rain.*

rebel[1] (*say* ri-bell)
to decide not to obey the people in charge   *The soldiers rebelled.*

rebel[2] (*say* reb-el)
someone who rebels

recall   to remember   *The old man could clearly recall his school-days.*

receive   to get something that has been given or sent to you   *Did you receive a letter this morning?*

recent   made or done a short time ago   *A recent record by this group was very popular.*

recipe   (*say* re-si-pee)
instructions that tell you how to cook something

recite   to say a poem or something else that you have learnt by heart

reckless   likely to do silly or dangerous things. Reckless people do things without thinking or caring about what might happen.

reckon   **1** to count or add up   *She quickly reckoned the cost of repairing the window.*
2 to think something and feel sure it is right   *I reckon that with all our skill our team should win.*

recognize   to know who someone is because you have seen them before

record   **1** a flat, round piece of black plastic that makes music or other sounds while it is turning round on a record-player
2 the best that has been done so far in a sport or hobby   *He broke the world record in that race.*
3 to put music or other sounds on a tape or disc

recorder   a wooden or plastic musical instrument shaped like a tube, that you blow

recorder

record-player a machine that makes sounds come out of records

recover **1** to get better after being ill
2 to get something back that you have lost *He recovered the bag that he had left on the bus.*

recreation hobbies or games people like playing in their spare time

rectangle the shape of a postcard

reduce to make smaller or less *She reduced speed as she got near the roundabout.*

reed a large grass with a strong stem that grows near water

reef a line of rocks just below or just above the surface of the sea

reek to have a strong smell that is not pleasant *The room reeked of stale cigarette smoke.*

reel

reel **1** a round piece of wood or metal that cotton, string, fishing line, or film is wound round *Put a new reel of film in the camera.*
2 a Scottish dance
3 to lose your balance because you feel dizzy

refer **1** to say a little about something while talking about other things
2 to look in a book for information or facts

referee someone who makes sure that the players in a game keep to the rules

reference book a book that gives you information. Dictionaries are reference books.

reflect **1** to send back light from a shiny surface. Water often reflects the light of the sun.
2 to show a picture of something, as a mirror does *The trees were reflected in the clear water.*

reflection a picture seen in a mirror or water

refresh to make a tired person feel fresh and strong again *a refreshing drink*

refreshments drinks and snacks

refrigerator a kind of metal cupboard that keeps food and drink cold and fresh, often called a **fridge**

refuse¹ (*say* ri-<u>fuse</u>)
1 to say you will not do something you have been asked to do *She refused to tidy her room.*
2 to say you do not want what someone is offering you *He refused a third cream-cake.*

refuse² (*say* <u>ref</u>-yooss)
rubbish

regard to think of someone or something in a certain way *He regarded the football player as his hero.*

regiment a large, organized group of soldiers

region a part of a country or the world *Snow covers the northern regions of the earth all year round.*

register an important book with a list of names and addresses in it *a school register*

regret the feeling you have when you are sorry about something *She regretted she had been cross when she saw he was upset.*

regular **1** usual
2 always happening at certain times *regular meals*

rehearsal a practice for a concert or play

rehearse to practise something before it is done in front of an audience

reign 1 to be king or queen *You will reign over the land for the rest of your life.*
2 the time when someone is king or queen *Many changes took place during her reign.*

reindeer a kind of deer that lives in very cold countries

reindeer

reins the two long straps used for guiding a horse

rejoice to be very happy about something *The school rejoiced at their team's success.*

relation a relative

relative someone in the same family as you

relax to rest the body by letting it become less stiff *She relaxed in the warm bath.*

relay race a race between teams in which each person does part of the distance

release to set someone free

relent to be less angry than you were going to be *She relented and let them watch the programme.*

reliable able to be trusted *a reliable person*

relic something very old that was left by people who lived long ago

relief the feeling you have when you are no longer in trouble, pain, or danger

relieved happy because you are no longer in trouble, pain, or danger *They were relieved to see the helicopter coming to rescue them.*

religion what people believe about God and the way they worship

reluctant not willing to do something *He was reluctant to set off as it was raining.*

rely to trust someone or something to help you *The blind man relied on his dog.*

remain 1 to stay *The sign remained long after the circus had gone.*
2 to be left behind *Very little food remained after their picnic.*

remainder what is left over *Ten children went swimming. The remainder played tennis.*

remark to say something that you have thought or noticed

remarkable so unusual that you remember it

remedy something that cures an illness *An old remedy for curing warts is supposed to be counting them.*

relay race

remember to be able to bring something into your mind when you want to

remind to make or help someone remember something

remote far away *Does your T.V. have remote control?*

removal van a van for moving the things inside a house to a different house

remove to take something away

rent an amount of money paid every week or month for the use of something that belongs to another person

repair to mend *She repaired the hole in the roof.*

repeat to say or do the same thing again

repent to be very sorry about something you have said or done *She repented, after being unkind.*

replace **1** to put something back *He replaced the book on the shelf.* **2** to take the place of another person or thing *We have a new car to replace the old one.*

reply to answer *You must reply to her letter.*

report to tell or write news

represent **1** to speak or do things in place of another person or a group of people *The girls represented the school in the competition.* **2** to be a picture or model of something *This picture represents our school last century.*

reptile an animal with cold blood that creeps or crawls. Snakes, crocodiles, and tortoises are all reptiles.

reputation the things everyone says or thinks about a person

request to ask politely for something

a remote control

require to need

rescue to save from danger

resemble to look or sound like another person or thing *He resembled his father.*

reserve **1** to keep for later *She reserved some seeds to plant next year.* **2** someone ready to take part in a game if a member of the team cannot play *The reserve waited at the side of the pitch.*

reptiles

chameleon

viper

gecko

reservoir a place where a very large amount of water is stored

resist to fight against something and not give way *He resisted all their attempts to make him change his mind.*

resolve to decide *She resolved to try harder at dancing.*

respect the feeling you have for someone you like and admire

responsible in charge and likely to take the blame if anything goes wrong

rest **1** to lie down, lean against something, or sit without doing anything
2 the part that is left *Eat as much as you can: the dog can have the rest.*
3 the other people or things *You stay, but the rest can go.*

restaurant a place where you can buy a meal and eat it

restore to make something as good as it was before *The ruined church was restored.*

result **1** anything that happens because of other things that have happened
2 the score or marks at the end of a game, competition, or test

retire to stop working because you are too old or ill *My grandmother is retiring soon.*

retreat to go back because it is too dangerous to carry on

return **1** to come back to a place
2 to give something back

reveal to let something be seen or known *He moved the paper and revealed the presents.*

revenge a wish to hurt someone because they have hurt you or one of your friends

reverse **1** the opposite side or way
2 to go backwards in a car

revolt **1** to say that you will not obey the people in charge
2 *revolting* so nasty that you feel sick

revolution a great struggle to get rid of the government by force and put a new kind of government in its place

revolver a small gun that can be fired several times without having to be loaded again

reward a present given to someone because of something they have done

rhinoceros a very large, heavy animal found in Africa and Asia. Rhinoceroses have horns on their noses.

rhubarb a plant with pink stalks that are cooked and eaten with sugar

rhyme (*say* rime)
A word that has the same sound at the end as another word. *Bat* and *mat* are rhymes and so are *batter* and *matter*.

rhythm (*say* ri-them)
the pattern made in music or poetry by the strong and weak sounds

rib one of the curved bones above the waist

ribbon a strip of nylon, silk, or some other material

rice shiny white seeds that are cooked in liquid. The seeds come from a kind of grass grown in marshes in hot countries.
rice pudding

rice plants

rich having a lot of money

rick a neat pile of straw or hay

ridden see ride

riddle a question or puzzle that is a joke, such as *Why do Swiss cows have bells?* Because their horns don't work.

ride **1** to sit on a horse or bicycle and control it as it moves along *Have you ridden before? I rode her pony yesterday Do you like riding?* **2** to travel in a car, bus, or train

ridge a long, narrow part higher than the rest, like the line along the top of a roof

ridiculous so silly that people might laugh at it *a ridiculous answer*

rifle a long gun that is held against the shoulder when it is fired

right **1** on the side opposite the left. Most people hold a knife in their right hand and a fork in their left hand. **2** correct *the right answer* **3** fair *It is not right to cheat.* **4** completely *Turn it right round.*

right-handed using the right hand to write and do other important things, because you find it easier than using the left hand

rim the edge round the top of a round container or round the outside of a wheel

rind the skin on bacon, cheese, or fruit

ring **1** a circle **2** a circle of thin metal worn on the finger **3** to make a bell sound **4** to telephone *He rang up the police an hour ago.*

ring-master the person with a top hat and a whip who is in charge of what happens in the circus ring

rink an area of ice or ground for skating on

rinse to wash something in clean water

riot a large group of people shouting and fighting

rip to tear

ripe ready to be gathered or eaten

ripen to become ripe *The fruit will ripen in the sun.*

ripple a tiny movement on the surface of water

rise **1** to go upwards *The sun has already risen. Prices are rising.* **2** to get up *They all rose as she came in.*

risk the chance of danger

rival someone trying to win the same prize as you are

river a large stream

road a way with a hard surface made for people, animals, and traffic to go along

roam to move around without trying to get anywhere *They roamed all over the hills.*

roar to make the loud, deep sound a lion makes

roast to cook meat or vegetables inside the oven with fat

robber someone who steals and is ready to hurt people who get in their way

robbery taking things by force from other people *a bank robbery*

robin a small, brown bird with a red patch on its front

robot a machine that can move and behave like a person

rock **1** something very hard and heavy that is part of the mountains, the hills, and the ground **2** a hard sweet shaped like a stick and sold at the seaside **3** to move gently backwards and forwards or from side to side

rocket **1** a firework joined to a stick. Rockets shoot high into the air when they are lit.
2 a tall metal tube that is used to launch spacecraft. Hot gases rush out of it at the bottom and the spacecraft takes off.

rocket 2

rod a long, thin, round piece of wood or metal

rode see **ride**

rogue someone who is not honest

roll **1** a cylinder made by rolling something up
2 a very small loaf of bread
3 to turn over and over like a ball moving along the ground

roller **1** a heavy cylinder rolled over things to make them flat or smooth *a road roller*
2 a small cylinder put in hair to curl it *a hair roller*

roller-boot a set of small wheels that are fitted into a boot and make you able to move quickly and smoothly over the ground

rolling-pin a wooden cylinder rolled over pastry to make it flat

roof the part that covers the top of a building

room **1** one of the spaces with walls round it inside a building. Bathrooms, kitchens, and lounges are rooms.
2 enough space for something

roost the place where a bird rests at night

root the part of a plant that grows under the ground

rope a lot of strong threads twisted together

rose **1** a flower with a sweet smell and thorns on its stem
2 see **rise**

rosy coloured like a pink or red rose

rot to go soft or bad so that it cannot be used. Fruit and wood rot.

rotten **1** very bad *a rotten player*
2 so soft or bad that it cannot be used *a rotten apple, rotten wood*

rough **1** not smooth *rough wood*
2 not gentle *a rough boy*
3 not exact *a rough guess*

round **1** shaped like a circle or ball
2 on all sides of something *a fence round the field*

roundabout **1** a machine with seats that moves round and round. People can ride on roundabouts at fairs or in parks.
2 a place where roads meet and all traffic has to go round in the same direction

roller boots

rounders a game played outside between two teams with a small ball and a bat like a heavy stick

rouse to wake someone up

route (*say* root)
the way you have to go to get to a place

row¹ (*rhymes with* toe)
1 people or things in a straight line
The class stood in two rows.
2 to use oars to make a boat move
He rowed the boat across the river.

row² (*rhymes with* how)
1 a quarrel
2 a lot of noise

royal belonging to a king or queen
the royal family

rubber **1** a strong material that stretches, bends, and bounces. Rubber is used for making tyres, balls, elastic bands, and many other things.
2 a piece of rubber for rubbing out pencil marks

rubbish **1** things that are not wanted or needed
2 nonsense *You're talking rubbish!*

ruby a red jewel

rudder a flat part fixed to the end of a ship or aeroplane and used to steer it

rude not polite

rugged (*say* rug-id)
rough and full of rocks *rugged countryside*

ruin **1** to spoil something completely
The rain ruined the corn.
2 a building that has fallen down *The castle was now a ruin.*

rule **1** something that everyone ought to obey
2 to be in charge of a country and the people who live there
3 to draw a straight line with a ruler

ruler **1** someone who rules a country or empire
2 a strip of wood, metal, or plastic with straight edges, used for measuring and drawing straight lines

rumble to make the deep, heavy sound thunder makes

rumour something that a lot of people are saying, although it might not be true

run to use the legs to move quickly
He saw the bull and ran.

rung **1** one of the short bars on a ladder
2 see **ring**

rush to move very quickly

rusk a kind of biscuit for babies

rust a rough, red surface that covers iron that has got damp or wet *The old car was covered in rust.*

rustle to make the light sounds dry leaves make when they are blown by the wind

rut a groove made in the ground by wheels going over it many times

rye a plant grown by farmers. Its seed is used for feeding animals and making some kinds of bread.

S s

sabbath the day of the week that is set aside for rest and prayer. For some people the sabbath is Saturday but for many others it is Sunday.

sack **1** a large bag made of strong, rough material *a sack of potatoes*
2 *to get the sack* to lose your job

sacred very holy

sacrifice **1** to give up something you like very much in order to help someone
2 a gift offered to God

saddle a seat put on a horse's back or on a bicycle so that you can ride it

safari a journey made by people in order to hunt or look at lions and other wild animals

safe **1** free from danger
2 a strong box where money or valuable things can be kept safe from thieves

safety a time or place free from danger
The fireman carried her to safety.

sag to go down in the middle because something heavy is pressing on it
The chair sagged under his weight.

said see **say**

sail **1** a large piece of strong cloth joined to a boat. The wind blows into the sail and makes the boat move
2 to travel in a boat

sailor a member of a ship's crew

saint a very holy person *St. Nicholas*

sake *for someone's sake* to help or please someone *Please do it for my sake.*

salad a mixture of vegetables eaten raw or cold

salary money paid to someone each month for the work they do

sale **1** the selling of things *These toys are not for sale.*
2 a time when things in a shop are sold at reduced prices *The shoe shop is having a sale.*

salmon a large fish with pink flesh that is eaten

salt a white powder put on food to give it flavour

salute to touch your forehead with your hand, as soldiers do to show respect

same not different in any way

sample a small amount that shows what something is like

sand the tiny bits of rock that cover deserts and ground next to the sea

sandal a kind of light shoe with a sole and straps that go round the foot

sandwich two slices of bread and butter with a different food between them

sang see **sing**

sank see **sink**

sap the liquid inside a plant

sapling a young tree

sardine a small sea fish you can eat

sari a kind of long dress worn by Indian women and girls

sash a strip of material tied round the waist of a dress

sat see **sit**

satchel a bag worn over the shoulder or on the back, for carrying books to and from school

satellite something that moves in space around earth or another planet. The moon is a satellite of the earth.

satellite

129

satin   smooth cloth that is very shiny on one side

satisfactory   good enough   *satisfactory work*

satisfy   to be good enough to please someone   *Nothing satisfies him – he's always complaining.*

sauce   a thick liquid put on food to make it taste better

saucepan   a metal pan with a handle and lid used for cooking things on top of a stove

saucer   a kind of small plate for putting a cup on

sausage   a skin tube stuffed with tiny pieces of meat and bread

savage   wild and fierce   *a savage animal*

save   **1** to free someone or something from danger
2 to keep something so that it can be used later

saw   **1** a tool with a wide, thin blade that is moved backwards and forwards across a piece of wood to cut it
2 to use a saw to cut a piece of wood   *The wood was sawn in two.*
I sawed it in half yesterday.
3 see see

saws

sawdust   a powder that comes from wood when it is cut with a saw

sawed, sawn   see saw

say   to use the voice to make words   *He said he hadn't seen it.*

saying   something wise that is often said, such as 'A stitch in time saves nine.'

scab   hard, brown skin that covers a cut or graze while it is getting better

scabbard   a cover for the blade of a sword

scaffolding   planks fixed to poles and put round a building so that workmen can stand on them while they are painting or mending it

scald   to burn yourself with very hot liquid

scales   **1** a weighing machine   *a pair of scales*
2 thin pieces of skin or bone that cover the outside of animals such as fish and snakes

scalp   the skin covering the top of the head where the hair grows

scamper   to run about quickly. Small dogs scamper.

scar   the mark left on the skin by a cut or burn after it has healed

scarce   **1** not enough of something   *Water is scarce in deserts.*
2 not often seen or found   *Adders are scarce in this country.*

scare   to frighten   *Stop scaring me!*

scarecrow   something that looks like a person and is put in a field to frighten away birds so that they will not eat the crops

scarf   a piece of material worn round the neck or head   *two scarves*

scarlet   bright red

scatter   to throw small things so that they fall in many different places

scene   **1** the place where something happens   *the scene of the crime*
2 part of a play

scooter 2

scenery **1** painted curtains and screens put on a stage to make it look like another place
2 things such as hills, rivers, and trees that you can see around you when you are out in the country

scent **1** a liquid with a sweet smell
2 a pleasant smell   *the scent of roses*
3 an animal's smell   *a fox's scent*

scholarship money given to someone clever in order to help them to go on studying

school the place where children go to learn

science knowledge about the world that people get by studying things and testing ideas about the way they work

scientific having to do with science   *a scientific experiment*

scientist someone who studies science

scissors a tool for cutting that has two blades joined together   *a pair of scissors*

scoff to make fun of something   *They scoffed at his boast that he could swim across the river.*

scold to tell someone off angrily   *He scolded the child for picking the flowers.*

scoop **1** a deep spoon for lifting up and measuring out potato or ice cream
2 to use a tool or your arms or hands to gather things together and lift them up

scooter **1** a toy with two wheels that is ridden. You stand on it with one foot and push the other foot against the ground to make it move.
2 a kind of motorbike with a very small engine

scorch to make something so hot that it goes brown   *The sun scorched the grass.*

score **1** to get a goal or point in a game
2 the number of points or goals each side has at the end of a game
3 twenty   *three score years and ten*

scorn to show that you think someone or something is not worth bothering about   *He scorned their offers of help.*

scorpion a kind of spider with a poisonous sting in its tail.

scout a soldier sent to spy on the enemy

Scout a boy who is a member of the Scout Association

scowl to make your face look unhappy and angry

scramble **1** to use your hands and feet to climb up or down something
2 *scrambled eggs* eggs mixed with milk and cooked in butter

scrap **1** a small piece   *A scrap of material will make a doll's dress.*
2 rubbish   *That pile of wood is all scrap.*

scrape to rub with something rough or sharp

scratch **1** to damage something by rubbing your nails or a sharp point over it
2 to rub your skin to stop it itching

scrawl to write with big, untidy letters

scream to make a loud cry that shows that you are very frightened or in pain

screech to make a loud, shrill sound that is not pleasant. Some owls screech.

screen **1** a smooth surface on which films or television programmes are shown
2 a kind of thin wall or a set of curtains on rails, that can be moved about. Screens are used for hiding things or protecting people.

seals 1

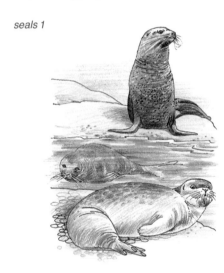

screw **1** a kind of nail that is put into a hole and twisted in order to fasten things tightly together
2 to turn or twist something

screwdriver a tool for turning a screw until it fits tightly into something

scribble to write or draw quickly and untidily

scripture the Bible

scroll a book written on a long sheet of paper that is rolled up

scrub to rub something very hard with a brush dipped in soap and water

sculptor an artist who makes shapes and patterns in stone, wood, clay, or metal

scurry to run with fast, little steps. Mice scurry.

scuttle **1** to move quickly like a frightened mouse
2 a kind of bucket in which coal is kept

scythe (*say* sythe)
a tool with a long curved blade for cutting grass

sea a very large area of salt water

sea-gull a kind of sea bird

seal **1** a furry animal that lives in the sea and on land
2 to close something by sticking two parts together *a sealed envelope*

seam the line where two pieces of cloth are sewn together

search to look very carefully for something

searchlight a strong light that can be pointed in any direction

seaside a place by the sea where people go to enjoy themselves

season **1** one of the four parts of the year. Spring, summer, autumn, and winter are the names of the seasons.
2 to put herbs or spices on food to make it taste better

seat a chair or stool or anything else that people sit on

seaweed a plant that grows in the sea

second **1** a very small measure for time *60 seconds = 1 minute*
2 coming after the first *second prize*

secret something that must be kept hidden from other people

secretary someone whose job is to type letters, answer the telephone, and arrange things in an office

section a part of something *This section of the book is very interesting.*

secure safe or firm *Make sure the ladder is secure before you climb it.*

see to use your eyes to get to know something *I saw an accident this morning. Have you seen my cat anywhere?*

seed a tiny thing put into the ground so that a plant can grow from it

seek to try to find *We sought for him everywhere, but could not find him.*

seem to make people think something is true or likely

seen see **see**

see-saw a plank balanced in the middle so that someone can sit on each end and make it go up and down

see-saw

seize to take hold of something suddenly *The cat seized the toy mouse.*

seldom not often *I seldom cry.*

select to choose

self everything in a person that makes them different from anyone else

selfish only bothered about yourself and what you want

sell to give in return for money *I sold my bike yesterday.*

semicircle half of a circle

semi-colon a mark like this

send to make a person or thing go somewhere *She sent me a card last week.*

senior older or more important

sensation 1 anything that you can feel happening to yourself *The cold water gave me a tingling sensation in my feet.*
2 something very exciting that happens

sense 1 the power to see, hear, smell, feel, or taste
2 the ability to know what it is best to do or say *She used her common sense and called an ambulance.*

sensible wise *a sensible person a sensible idea*

sensitive easily hurt or offended *sensitive skin a sensitive person*

sent see **send**

sentence a group of words that belong together. A written sentence always begins with a capital letter and ends with a question mark like this ?, an exclamation mark like this !, or a full stop like this *Is this a sentence? Yes, it is.*

sentry a soldier who is guarding a building

separate not joined to anything

sequin one of the tiny, round, shiny things sewn on clothes to decorate them

sergeant a policeman or soldier who is in charge of other policemen or soldiers

serial a story told in parts *a television serial*

series 1 a full set *a series of stamps*
2 a number of things that are similar and come one after the other *a television series*

serious   **1** careful and thoughtful
a serious boy
2 not silly or funny   *a serious talk*
3 very bad   *a serious accident*

serpent   a large snake

servant   someone whose job is to work in someone else's house

serve   **1** to work for someone
2 to sell things to people in a shop
3 to give food out at a meal

serviette   a square of cloth or paper for keeping you clean while you eat

session   a time spent doing one thing
We had a training session at the sports centre.

set   **1** a group of people or things that belong together   *a set of drums*
2 to become solid or hard   *The jelly has set very quickly.*
3 to put
4 *to set off*   to start   *They set off for home.*

settee   a long, comfortable seat with a back, for more than one person

settee

settle   **1** to get comfortable in a place and stay there   *We're settling down in our new home now.*
2 to decide   *We've settled on the colour of the paint.*

several   more than a few but not a lot

severe   **1** not kind or gentle   *a severe teacher*
2 very bad   *a severe cold*

sew   (*say* so)
to use a needle and cotton to join pieces of cloth together   *He has sewn his badge on.*

sex   one of the two groups, either male or female, that all people and animals belong to

shabby   looking worn and faded
shabby clothes

shack   a rough hut

shade   **1** a place that is darker and cooler than other places, because the light of the sun cannot get to it
2 how light or dark a colour is
3 to make part of a drawing darker than the rest

shadow   the dark shape that you see on the wall or ground near something that is standing in the way of the light

shaft   **1** a long, thin pole   *the shaft of an arrow*
2 a deep, narrow hole   *a mine shaft*

shaggy   with long, untidy hair
a shaggy dog

shake   to move quickly up and down or from side to side   *I shook with fear, when I saw it.*

shallow   not deep   *shallow water*

shame   the feeling you have when you are upset because you have done wrong

shameful   so bad that it brings you shame   *shameful behaviour*

shampoo   liquid soap used for washing hair

shape   the pattern that a line drawn round the outside of something makes. A ball has a round shape.

share   **1** to make something into parts and give them out to other people   *She shared out the cake.*
2 to use something that someone else is also using   *Can I share your book?*

shark

shark　a large sea fish with sharp teeth

sharp　**1** with an edge or point that can cut or make holes　*a sharp knife*
2 sudden　*a sharp bend in the road*
3 quick to notice things or learn　*sharp eyes, a sharp boy*

shatter　to break suddenly into tiny pieces

shave　to cut hair from the skin to make it smooth. Men shave their faces.

shawl　a piece of cloth or knitting worn round the shoulders or wrapped round a baby

sheaf　a bundle of corn stalks tied together at harvest time　*three sheaves*

garden shears

shears　a tool like a very large pair of scissors for cutting plants or grass, or for clipping wool from sheep

sheath　a cover for the sharp blade of a sword or knife

sheaves　more than one **sheaf**

shed　**1** a small hut
2 to let something fall. Trees shed leaves, people shed tears, and caterpillars shed their skins.

sheep　an animal kept by farmers for its wool and meat　*two sheep*

sheer　very steep because it is straight up and down like a wall　*a sheer cliff*

sheet　**1** one of the large pieces of cloth put on a bed
2 a whole piece of paper, glass, or metal

shelf　a long piece of wood fastened to a wall, for putting things on　*two shelves*

shell　**1** the thin, hard part round an egg, a nut, and some kinds of animals, such as snails
2 a very large bullet that explodes when it hits something

shelter　a place that protects people from wind, rain, cold, or danger　*a bus shelter*

shelves　more than one **shelf**

shepherd　someone whose job is to look after sheep

sheriff　a man in charge of the law in a county or district

shield　a large piece of metal, leather, or wood used for protecting someone. Soldiers long ago held shields in front of themselves while they were fighting.

shields

shift to move something *Help me shift the table.*

shilling a British coin that was worth the same as 5p.

shimmer to shine with a light that comes and goes, like the light of the sun on water

shin the front of the leg between the knee and ankle

shine **1** to give out light *The sun shone all day.*
2 to look very bright *He polished it until it shone.*

shingle a lot of small stones by the edge of the sea

shiny with a surface that shines

ship a large boat that takes people or things on long journeys over the sea

shipwreck a bad accident that destroys or sinks a ship while it is at sea

shirk to get out of doing something that you ought to do *He was always shirking his turn to do the dishes.*

shirt a piece of clothing for the top half of the body with sleeves, a collar, and buttons down the front

shiver to shake because you are cold or frightened

shoal a large number of fish swimming together

shock a big surprise that is not pleasant

shoe a strong covering for the foot, with a stiff sole and heel *leather shoes*

shone see **shine**

shook see **shake**

shoot **1** to use a gun or a bow and arrow
2 to hurt or kill by shooting *A sheriff shot Billy the Kid.*
3 to move very quickly
4 to kick, hit, or throw a ball at the goal
5 a part of a plant that has just grown

shop **1** a place that people go into to buy things
2 to go to a shop to buy something

shore the land along the edge of the sea

short **1** not long *a short visit*
2 not tall *a short person*

shorthand

shorthand a set of signs for writing words down as quickly as people say them

shorts trousers that only cover the top part of the legs

shot **1** see **shoot**
2 the firing of a gun

should ought to *You should be working.*

shoulder the part of the body between the neck and arm

shout to speak very loudly

shove to push hard

shovel a kind of curved spade for lifting things such as coal or sand

show **1** to let something be seen *Show me your new bike.*
2 to make something clear to someone *He's shown me how to do it*
3 singing, dancing, and acting done to entertain people
4 things that have been put together and arranged so that people can come and look at them
a flower show

shower **1** a short fall of rain or snow
2 a lot of small things falling like rain
a shower of stones
3 *to have a shower* to stand under a spray of water and wash yourself

shown see **show**

shrank see **shrink**

shred a tiny strip of piece that has been cut, broken, or torn off something

shriek a short scream

shrill sounding very high and loud
a shrill whistle

shrimp a small sea creature with a shell

shrimps

shrink to become smaller *It shrank when it was washed. These jeans have shrunk.*

shrivel to get very dry and curl up at the edges like a dead leaf

shrub a bush

shrunk see **shrink**

shudder to shake suddenly because you are very cold or frightened

shuffle to drag your feet along the ground as you walk

shunt to move a train on to a different line

shut to move a cover, lid, or door in order to block up an opening

shutter **1** a wooden cover that fits over a window
2 the part inside a camera that opens to let in light as you take a photograph

shutters 1

shy **1** not willing to meet other people because you are afraid
2 easily frightened *a shy animal*

sick **1** ill
2 *to be sick* to bring food back up from the stomach through the mouth

side **1** one of the outer parts between the front and back of a person, animal, or thing
2 a flat surface *A cube has six sides.*
3 an edge *A triangle has three sides.*
4 a group playing or fighting against another group

sideboard a long, heavy piece of furniture with drawers, cupboards, and a flat top where things can be put

sideways **1** with the side first *The piano will fit through the door if you carry it sideways.*
2 to one side *He moved sideways to avoid the puddle.*

siege (*say* seej)
a time when the enemy surrounds a town or castle so that people and things cannot get in or out

sigh to breathe out heavily to show you are feeling very sad or very happy

sight 1 the ability to see *You are lucky to have good sight.*
2 something that is seen *He was a funny sight in that hat.*

sign 1 anything written, drawn, or done to tell or show people something *road signs*
2 to write your name in your own writing

signal a sound or movement that tells people something without words *traffic signals*

signature your name written by yourself in your own writing

silence a time when there is no sound at all

silent without any sound

silk very fine, shiny cloth made from threads spun by insects called **silk-worms**

sill a ledge underneath a window

silly not clever or careful *a silly person, a silly idea*

silver a valuable, shiny white metal

similar like another person or thing *Your dress is similar to mine.*

simple 1 easy *a simple question*
2 plain *a simple dress*
3 not complicated

since 1 from that time *We have been friends since last summer.*
2 because *An outing was not organized since few people wanted to go.*

sincere truly meant *sincere good wishes*

sing to use the voice to make a tune with sounds or words *We have sung this before. She sang a solo yesterday.*

singe to burn something slightly

single 1 only one *The tree has a single apple.*
2 not married

sink 1 a place with taps where you do the washing-up
2 to go under water *The ship sank last night. It has sunk.*
3 to go down

sip to drink a very small amount at a time

sir 1 a word used when speaking politely to a man, instead of his name
2 a title given to knights *Sir Winston Churchill*

siren a machine that makes a loud sound like a scream to warn people about something

sister a girl or woman who has the same parents as another person

sit to rest on your bottom, as you do when you are on a chair *She sat on the chair and broke it. Are you sitting comfortably?*

site the ground where something has been built or will be built

situation 1 the place where something is
2 the things that are happening to you

size 1 how big something is
2 the measurement something is made in *size ten shoes*

sizzle to make the noise sausages make when they are being fried

skate 1 a steel blade joined to the sole of a boat and used for moving smoothly over ice
2 to move smoothly over ice or the ground wearing skates or roller-skates

skateboard a long piece of wood or plastic on wheels. You balance on it with both feet while it moves quickly over the ground.

skeleton   the framework of bones inside the body

sketch   to draw quickly

ski   a long piece of metal and plastic strapped to the foot for moving quickly and smoothly over snow   *a pair of skis*

skid   to slide without meaning to *The car skidded on the wet road.*

skill   the ability to do something very well

skim   **1** to take the cream off the top of milk
2 to move quickly over the surface of something and only just touch it

skin   **1** the outer covering of the body
2 the outer covering of some fruits and vegetables

skip   **1** to move lightly and quickly by hopping from one foot to the other
2 to jump over a rope that is turning
3 to miss out   *Skip the next page.*

skipper   the person in charge of a ship or a team

skirt   a piece of clothing for women and girls that hangs down from the waist

skittle   one of a set of pieces of wood or plastic shaped like bottles that people try to knock down with a ball

skull   the bony framework inside the head

sky   the space overhead where the sun, moon, and stars can be seen

skylark   a small, brown bird that sings while flying high in the air

skateboard

skyscraper   a very tall, modern building

slab   a flat, thick piece   *a slab of toffee*

slack   **1** not pulled tight   *a slack rope*
2 careless   *slack work*
3 not busy   *a slack day*

slain   see

slam   to close something loudly

slanting   in a line that is higher at one end than the other, like the side of a triangle or a hill

slap   to hit with the flat part of your hand

slash   to make long cuts in something

slate   one of the thin pieces of smooth, grey rock used to cover a roof

slaughter
the killing of many people or animals

slave   someone who belongs to another person and has to work without wages

slay   to kill   *The dragon was slain. St. George slew the dragon.*

sled, sledge   something used for travelling over snow with strips of metal or wood, or a smooth base, instead of wheels

sledge

sleek   neat, smooth, and shiny

sleep   to close your eyes and rest completely, as you do every night *I slept in a tent last night.*

sleet   a mixture of rain and snow

sleeve   the part of a coat, shirt, blouse, or jersey, that covers the arm

sleigh   (*rhymes with* play) something used for travelling over snow. Sleighs are pulled by animals and have strips of wood or metal instead of wheels.

sleigh

slender   thin   *a slender girl*

slept   see **sleep**

slew   see **slay**

slide   **1** to move very quickly and smoothly over something
2 very slippery ground or a long, sloping piece of shiny metal that people can slide on
3 something pretty that girls put in their hair to keep it tidy
4 a small photograph that can be shown on a screen

slight   **1** small   *a slight cold*
2 thin
a very slight person

slim   **1** thin
2 to try to get thinner by eating less
My father is slimming.

slime   wet, slippery stuff that is not pleasant

sling   **1** a piece of cloth wrapped round an injured arm and tied round the neck so that it supports the arm
2 a short leather strap used for throwing stones

slink   to move in a secret way because you are afraid or feel guilty about something   *The dog saw me watching and slunk away.*

slip   **1** slide out of place
2 to fall over   *He slipped on some ice.*
3 to go away quickly and quietly
She slipped out of the room when the baby fell asleep.

slipper   a soft, comfortable kind of shoe worn indoors

slippery   with a very smooth surface so that it is difficult to get hold of or walk on

slit   a long cut or a narrow opening in something

slop   to make a mess by letting liquid run over the edge of a container   *The bucket was so full that some water slopped out.*

slope   **1** ground that is like the side of a hill   *It's hard to run up a steep slope.*
2 to be slanting   *Does the roof slope or is it flat?*

slot   a narrow opening for something like a coin to fit into   *Put a coin in the slot and you'll get a ticket.*

slouch   to move, sit, or stand with the head and shoulders bent forwards
The tired pupil slouched at his desk.

slow   **1** taking more time than usual
a slow train
2 showing a time that is earlier than the correct time. Watches and clocks are sometimes slow.

sludge   thick, sticky mud

slug   a small creature like a snail without its shell

slum   an area of old, dirty, crowded houses

slumber   sleep

slunk   see **slink**

slush   melting snow

sly   clever at tricking people secretly

smack to hit with the flat part of the hand

small little *a small dog*

smart **1** dressed well *That hat looks very smart.*
2 neat and tidy *If you comb your hair, you'll look much smarter.*
3 clever *What a smart dog!*
4 to feel a stinging pain *The bee sting made his hand smart.*

smash to break into pieces with a loud noise

smear **1** to make a dirty mark by rubbing against something
2 to rub something over a surface

smell **1** to use the nose to find out about something *I bent down and smelt the rose.*
2 anything that can be smelt

smile to make your face show that you are happy

smith someone who makes things out of metal

smoke **1** blue or grey gas that floats up from a fire and looks like a cloud
2 to have a cigarette or pipe between the lips, take in the smoke from it, and breathe it out

smooth free from lumps or rough parts *a smooth surface*

smother **1** to cover thickly *a cake smothered in cream*
2 to cover someone's mouth and nose so that he cannot breathe

smoulder to burn slowly with a lot of smoke

smudge a dirty mark made by rubbing against something

smuggle to bring something into a country secretly without paying the tax that should be paid to the government

snack something you can eat quickly instead of a meal

snail a small creature that lives inside a shell. Snails are found on land and in water.

snails

snake a creature with a long body and no legs. Some snakes can give poisonous bites.

snap **1** to break suddenly
2 to bite suddenly *The horse snapped at his groom.*

snapshot a photograph

snare a trap for catching animals

snarl to make the sound a dog makes when it is angry

snatch to take something quickly

sneak **1** someone who tells tales
2 to move trying not to be seen or heard *She sneaked up behind him and made him jump.*

sneer to speak or smile in an insulting way that shows that you think someone is not worth bothering about

sneeze to make a sudden noise as air rushes out of the nose *I can't stop sneezing.*

sniff to make a noise by suddenly taking in air through the nose

snip to cut a little bit off something

snob someone who only bothers with people that they think are clever or important

snooker a game played on a long table with rods and twenty-two small, coloured balls

snooker

snore to breathe very noisily while sleeping

snorkel a tube for someone to breathe through while they are swimming under water

snorkel

snorkel

snout an animal's nose and mouth sticking out from the rest of its face. Pigs have snouts.

snow small, thin, white pieces of frozen water. Snow floats down from the sky when the weather is very cold.

snowdrop a small white flower that grows in January and February

snub to show someone who is trying to be friendly that you do not want to be their friend

snug cosy

snuggle to curl up in a warm, comfortable place *The kitten snuggled up to its mother.*

soak to make something very wet

soap something used with water for washing

soar to move high into the air *The eagle soared high above them.*

sock a covering for the foot and part of the leg

socket the part that an electric light bulb or plug fits into

sofa a long, comfortable seat with a back, for more than one person

soft 1 not firm. Cotton wool and wet clay are soft.
2 not loud

software the programs that are put into a computer

soggy wet through

soil the brown stuff on the ground, that plants grow in

solar anything to do with the sun *solar energy, the solar system*

sold see **sell**

soldier a member of the army

sole 1 the flat part underneath a foot or shoe
2 a sea fish that is eaten

solemn serious

solid 1 not hollow. A cricket ball is solid. A tennis ball is not.
2 firm. Liquids and gases are not solid. *solid rock*

solitary alone or lonely

solo something sung, played, danced, or done by one person

solution 1 the answer to a puzzle or problem
2 something dissolved in a liquid

solve   to find the answer to a puzzle

some   **1** a few   *some sweets*
2 a certain amount of   *some cake*
3 a, an, or one   *Some insect has just bitten me.*

somebody   a person

somehow   in some way

someone   a person

somersault   (*say* summer-solt)
1 a jump, turning head over heels in the air
2 a forward or backward roll on the ground

something   some thing

sometimes   at some times

somewhere   in some place or to some place

son   a boy or man who is someone's child

song   words that are sung

soon   in a very short time from now

soot   the black powder left behind by smoke

soothe   to make someone who is upset feel calm   *soothing words*

sorcerer   a man in fairy tales, who can do magic things

sorcerer

sore   painful when it is touched
sore skin

sorrow   a very sad feeling

sorry   **1** sad about something that you wish you had not done
2 sad because of something that has happened to another person

sort   **1** a kind   *I like this sort best.*
2 to arrange things into different groups

sought   see **seek**

soul   the part of a person that cannot be seen but is believed to go on living after they have died

sound   **1** anything that can be heard
2 to make a sound

soup   a hot liquid made from meat or vegetables

sour   **1** with the kind of taste lemons and vinegar have
2 not fresh   *sour milk*

source   the place something has come from   *The source of the river is up in the hills.*

south   the direction to your right when you face east

southern   from the south or in the south

souvenir   (*say* soo-ven-eer)
something that you keep because it makes you think about a person or place   *He brought back souvenirs from his holiday.*

sovereign   a ruler who is a king, queen, emperor, or empress

sow¹   (*rhymes with* toe)
to put seeds in the ground so that they will grow into plants   *The grain was sown in the spring.*

sow²   (*rhymes with* how)
a female pig

space **1** the distance between things **2** a place with nothing in it **3** all the places beyond the earth, where the stars and planets are. Outer space is so vast that it cannot be measured.

spacecraft any kind of vehicle that can travel in space

spaceship a machine that can carry people and things through space

space shuttle a spaceship designed to carry people and cargo from earth to a satellite and back

space shuttle

spade **1** a tool with a long handle and a short, wide blade for digging **2** a small, black spade printed on some playing-cards

spaghetti a food that looks like long pieces of string when it is cooked

span **1** to reach from one side of something to the other, as a bridge does **2** the distance between the top of the thumb and the top of the little finger when the hand is spread out

spaniel a kind of dog with silky fur and long ears

spank to hit someone hard on the bottom

spanner a tool that fits round a nut so that you can turn it to make it tighter or looser

spare **1** not used but kept in case it is needed *a spare tyre* **2** to give up something so that someone else can have it *Could you spare one of your pencils?*

spark **1** a tiny piece of burning stuff **2** a tiny flash

sparkle to shine with a lot of tiny flashes of bright light

sparkler a kind of firework that sparkles. You can hold it in your hand while it burns.

sparklers

sparrow a small, brown bird that is often seen in gardens

spat see **spit**

spawn the eggs of frogs, fish, and some other water creatures *We saw some frog spawn in the pond.*

speak to say something *She spoke to me yesterday.* *I've not spoken to him yet.*

spear a long pole or stick with a very sharp point, used as a weapon

spider

spice part of a plant such as the berry or seed that is dried and used in cooking to give food a stronger flavour. Ginger and pepper are spices.

spider a small creature with eight legs that sometimes weaves webs to catch insects

spike a thin piece of metal with a sharp point

spill to let something fall out of a container *The cat drank the spilt milk.*

spin **1** to turn round and round quickly *I spun round until I was dizzy.*
2 to make thread by twisting long, thin pieces of wool or cotton together

special **1** different from any other kind
2 for one person or thing *a special cake for my birthday*

specimen **1** a small amount of something that shows what the rest is like
2 an example of one kind of plant or animal *She showed them a specimen of an oak leaf.*

speck **1** a tiny mark
2 a tiny bit of dust

speckled with small, coloured spots. Some birds' eggs are speckled.

spectacles a pair of glasses

spectator someone watching a game or show

speech **1** the power of speaking
2 a talk given to a group of people *The headmaster made a speech to the parents.*

speed how quickly something moves or happens

spell **1** to write a word correctly *How is your name spelt?*
2 magic words that make things happen

spend **1** to use money to pay for things
2 to pass time *I spent yesterday at home.*

sphere (*say* sfear)
the shape of a ball

spinning-wheel

spinach (*say* spin-itch)
a vegetable with a lot of green leaves, which you cook to eat

spine **1** the long bone down the centre of your back
2 a thorn or prickle

spinning-wheel a machine for spinning thread. It is worked by the hand or foot.

spinster a woman who has not married

spiral **1** the shape of a line that keeps going round the same point in smaller and smaller or bigger and bigger curves, like the jam in a slice of Swiss roll
2 *a spiral staircase* a staircase that you go round and round as you climb up it

145

spire   a tall, pointed part on top of a church tower

spirit   **1** the part of a person that cannot be seen but is believed to go on living after they have died
2 a ghost
3 something that makes a person very brave and lively   *He was in high spirits on the morning of the race.*

spit   to send drops of liquid out of the mouth   *The cat spat when it saw the dog.*

spiteful   full of a wish to hurt someone by what you say or do

splash   **1** to make drops of water fly about as they do when you jump into water
2 the noise you make when you jump into water

splendid   **1** very good   *a splendid holiday*
2 looking very grand   *a splendid uniform*

splint   a straight piece of wood or metal that is tied to a broken arm or leg to hold it firm

splinter   a sharp bit of wood, glass, or metal

split   to break something into parts

spoil   **1** to make something less good or useful than it was   *The ink stain has spoilt my dress.*
2 to be too kind to a child so that they think they can always have what they want   *The little boy was very spoilt.*

spoke   **1** see **speak**
2 one of the wires or rods that go from the centre of a wheel to the rim

spoken   see **speak**

sponge   **1** a light, soft cake
2 something thick and soft with a lot of holes in it. Sponges soak up water and are used for washing.

sponsor   someone who gives money to a charity for something done by another person

spool   a round piece of wood or metal that cotton, string, or film is wound round

spoon   what you use for eating soup and pudding

sport   a game or something else that is usually done outside and exercises the body. Running, jumping, football, and netball are all sports.

spot   **1** a round mark
2 a small, round swelling on the skin
3 a place   *a good spot for a picnic*
4 to notice something   *She spotted the mistake at once.*

spotlight   a strong light that can shine on one small area

spout   the part of a container that is made like a pipe so that you can pour liquid out of it easily. Teapots and kettles have spouts.

sprain   to twist the wrist or ankle so that it swells and is painful

sprang   see **spring**

sprawl   to sit or lie with your arms and legs spread out

spray   to make tiny drops of liquid fall all over something

spread   **1** to stretch something out to its full size   *The bird spread its wings.*
2 to make something cover a surface   *She spread the cloth on the table.*

spring   **1** the part of the year when plants start to grow and the days are getting lighter and warmer
2 a place where water comes out of the ground
3 a piece of metal wound into rings so that it jumps back into shape after it has been pressed or stretched
4 to move suddenly upwards   *I sprang up and caught the ball.*

sprinkle to make a few tiny pieces or drops fall on something

sprint to run a short distance very quickly

sprout **1** to start to grow *The seeds soon sprouted.*
2 a vegetable that looks like a tiny cabbage *Brussels sprouts*

sprung see **spring**

spun see **spin**

spurt **1** to move like water shooting suddenly upwards *The water spurted out of the broken pipe.*
2 to go faster suddenly

spy **1** someone who works secretly to find out things about another person or country
2 to notice *I spy with my little eye . . .*

squabble to quarrel about something that is not important

square a flat shape with four straight sides that are all the same length

squash **1** to press something hard so that it goes out of shape
2 a drink made from fruit
3 a game played indoors with rackets and a small rubber ball

squat to sit on the ground with your knees bent and your bottom resting on your heels

squaw a female American Indian

squeak to make the tiny, shrill sound a mouse makes

squeal to make a long, shrill sound *The pig squealed as it ran.*

squeeze to press something between your hands or two other things

squid a sea creature with eight short arms and two very long ones

squirm to twist and turn the body about, like a worm *He squirmed to avoid his aunt's kiss.*

squirrel

squirrel a small animal with a very thick tail that lives in trees

squirt to come or squeeze suddenly out of something *Too much toothpaste squirted out. He squirted washing-up liquid into the water.*

stab to hit someone with the sharp, pointed end of a knife or sword

stable a building in which horses are kept

stack a neat pile

stadium a large place where people can watch sports and games

staff **1** a group of people who work together in an office, shop, or school
2 a thick stick for walking with

stag a male deer

stage **1** a raised floor in a hall or theatre, on which people act, sing, or dance to entertain other people
2 the point someone has reached in doing something *The baby is at the crawling stage.*

stagger to try to stand or walk but find it difficult to stay upright

stagnant not flowing or fresh *a pool of stagnant water*

stain a dirty mark made on something by liquid

stair one of a set of steps for going up or down inside a building

staircase a set of stairs and banisters

stake a thick, pointed stick *She used a stake to support the rose bush.*

stale not fresh *stale bread*

stalk 1 a thin stem
2 to walk in a stiff way that shows you are angry *She stalked away from the game.*
3 to move secretly to get close to an animal you are hunting

stall 1 a kind of small shop or a table that things are sold on. Markets have stalls.
2 a place for one animal in a stable or shed

stallion a male horse.

stammer to keep repeating the sounds at the beginning of words when you speak

stamp 1 to bang the foot heavily on the ground
2 a piece of sticky paper with a picture on it. People put stamps on letters and parcels to show that they have paid to post them.

stand 1 to be on your feet without moving *I stood there until they came.*
2 something made for putting things on *a cake stand, a hat stand*

standard 1 how good something is *a high standard of work*
2 a flag

stank see **stink**

stapler a small machine that fastens papers together by pressing little pieces of wire into them

star 1 one of the tiny, bright lights you see in the sky at night
2 a famous singer or actor

starch part of the food we eat, especially potatoes. It can be made into a powder or liquid and used for making clothes stiff.

stare to look at someone or something for a long time, without moving your eyes

starlings

starling a dark brown bird often seen in large flocks

start 1 to take the first steps in doing something *She has started going to Brownies.*
2 to make something happen *They have started a chess club at school.*

startle to make a person or animal very surprised and frightened *startling news*

starvation illness or death caused by great hunger

stapler

staples

starve to be very ill or die because you have not got enough food

state **1** how someone or something is
His clothes were in a dreadful state.
2 to say something important
The policeman stated that he saw the man steal the watch.
3 a country or part of a country
United States of America

statement words that say something important

station **1** a place where people get on or off trains
2 a building for policemen or firemen

statue a model of a person made in stone or metal

stay **1** to be in the same place
2 to live somewhere as a visitor

steady not shaking in any way
a steady voice, a steady hand

steak (*rhymes with* rake)
a thick slice of meat or fish

steal to take something that does not belong to you and keep it *A dog stole the meat yesterday. The jewels were stolen.*

steam very hot water that has turned into a vapour

steel a strong, shiny metal made from iron

steep sloping sharply *a steep hill*

stile

stile

steeple a tall, pointed tower on top of a church

steer to make a ship, car, or bicycle go in the direction you want

stem **1** the main part of a plant above the ground
2 the thin part that joins a leaf, flower, or fruit to the rest of the plant

step **1** the movement you make with your foot when you are walking, running, or dancing
2 a flat place where you can put your foot when you are going up or down something

stew **1** meat and vegetables cooked in liquid
2 to cook something slowly in liquid

stepfather a man who is married to your mother but is not your real father

stepmother a woman who is married to your father but is not your real mother

stern **1** the back end of a boat
2 severe or strict *The headmaster looked very stern.*

stick **1** a long, thin piece of wood
2 a long, thin piece of anything
a stick of liquorice
3 to become fastened or joined to things, as glue and mud do *The sweets were stuck to the bag.*
4 to press a sharp point into something
Stick a pin in the balloon and it will burst.

sticky able to stick to things. Glue, jam, and honey are all sticky.

stiff not easily bent *stiff cardboard*

stile a set of steps made to help people to get over a fence

still **1** not moving *Hold it still.*
2 the same now as before *He is still ill.*

stilts a pair of poles with which you can walk high above the ground

sting 1 a sharp part with poison on it that some animals and plants have *A nettle sting hurts.*
2 to hurt someone with a sting *A bee stung me yesterday.*

stink to have a very strong, bad smell *The stable was filthy and stank. It has always stunk like this.*

stir 1 to move a liquid or a soft mixture round with a spoon *He stirred the cake mixture.*
2 to start to move *After a long sleep the baby started to stir.*

stirrup the metal part that hangs down each side of a horse's saddle for you to put your foot in while you are riding

stitch 1 a loop of thread made by the needle in sewing
2 one of the loops of wool on a knitting needle
3 a sudden pain in the side. People sometimes get stitches when they have been running.

stoat a small, brown, furry animal with a long body that kills and eats mice, rats, birds, and rabbits

stoat

stock 1 a lot of things kept ready to be sold or used *This shop is selling old stock cheaply.*
2 a garden flower with a sweet smell

stocking a covering for the foot and leg worn next to the skin

stoke to put coal or wood on a fire to keep it burning

stole, stolen see **steal**

stomach the part in the middle of the body, where food goes when it is eaten

stone 1 rock
2 a small piece of rock
3 the hard seed in the middle of a cherry, plum, peach, or apricot
4 a measure for weight *She weighs 4 stone.*

stood see **stand**

stool a small seat without a back

stoop to bend the body forwards

stop 1 to end *At last the baby stopped crying.*
2 to come to rest *The bus stopped.*
3 to stay

stopper something that fits into the top of a bottle to close it

store 1 to keep things until they are needed *The spare pencils were stored in the cupboard.*
2 a large shop *This store sells everything.*

storey all the rooms on the same floor in a building

stork a large bird with very long legs and a long beak

stork

strawberries

storm   a very strong wind with a lot of rain or snow

story   words that tell you about something that has really happened or about something that someone has made up   *adventure stories*

stout   fat   *a stout lady*

stove   something that gives out heat for warming a room or for cooking

straight   **1** like a line drawn with a ruler   *a straight road*
2 *straight away* at once

straighten   **1** to make something straight
2 to become straight

strain   **1** to stretch, push, or try too hard
2 to hurt part of yourself by stretching or pushing too hard   *The football player strained his ankle.*
3 to separate a liquid from lumps or other things floating in it. People strain tea to get rid of the tea leaves.

strange   **1** not known or seen before   *a strange place*
2 unusual and very surprising   *a strange story*

stranger   **1** someone in a place he does not know
2 someone you do not know

strangle   to kill someone by pressing on their throat until they cannot breathe

strap   a flat strip of leather or another strong material for fastening things together

straw   **1** dry stalks of corn
2 a very thin tube for drinking through

strawberry   a small, red, juicy fruit   *strawberry jam*

stray   lost and without a home   *a stray cat*

streak   **1** a long, narrow mark   *The tears made streaks down her dirty face.*
2 to move very quickly   *The jet streaked across the sky.*

stream   a small river

streamer   a long strip of paper or a ribbon joined by one end to something to decorate it

street   a road with houses along each side

strength   how strong someone or something is

stretch   to pull something to make it longer, wider, or tighter

stretcher   a pair of poles with canvas stretched across them for carrying a sick or injured person

strict   keen on always being obeyed   *strict parents*

stride   to walk with long steps   *I strode angrily out of the room.*

strike   **1** to hit   *The house was struck by lightning.*
2 *to strike a match* to rub a match along something rough so that it bursts into flame
3 to stop working until the people in charge agree to make things better   *The women voted to strike for better working conditions*

string   very thin rope

strip   **1** a long, narrow piece   *She cut off a strip of paper.*
2 to take off clothes or a covering *He stripped off his clothes and jumped in the bath.*

stripe   a coloured band across or down something

strode   see **stride**

stroke   **1** to move the hand gently along something
2 a hitting movement   *We learnt a new tennis stroke.*

stroll   to walk slowly, because you are enjoying your walk and do not have to get anywhere

strong   **1** healthy and able to do things that need a lot of energy   *a strong horse*
2 not easily broken   *strong rope*
3 with a lot of flavour   *strong tea*

struck   see **strike**

structure   **1** anything that has been built
2 the way something has been built *The structure of the human body is very complicated.*

struggle   **1** to use your arms and legs in fighting or trying to get free *The thief struggled to get away from the police.*
2 to try very hard to do something you find difficult   *He struggled to improve his football skills.*

stubborn   not willing to change your ideas even though they might be wrong

stuck   see

stud   a small knob like the ones on the sole of a football boot

student   someone who studies at college or university

studio   a place where films or radio or television programmes are made

study   **1** to spend time learning about something   *We studied space travel in our project.*
2 to look at something very carefully *He studied the map looking for the place.*
3 a room where someone studies *The book is in the study.*

stuff   **1** anything used for making things
2 to fill something tightly
3 to push something inside another thing

stuffy   without fresh air   *a stuffy room*

stumble   to fall over something

stump   **1** the part of a broken tree, tooth, or pencil that is left
2 one of the set of three upright sticks put at each end of the pitch in cricket

stump 1

studio

stun **1** to hit or hurt someone so much that they cannot think properly
2 to make someone very surprised *She was stunned to receive so many presents.*

stung see **sting**

stunk see **stink**

stupid **1** very silly *a stupid idea*
2 slow to learn and understand

sturdy strong and healthy *a sturdy child*

stutter to keep repeating the sounds at the beginning of words when you speak

sty **1** a sore swelling on the edge of an eyelid
2 a place where pigs are kept *two sties*

style the way something is done or made *That is a neat style of writing.*

subject **1** the person or thing that you are writing about or learning about *What is the subject of your project?*
2 someone who is ruled by a king, queen, or government *We are all subjects of the Queen.*

submarine a ship that can travel under water

submarine

substance anything that can be seen, touched, or used for making things *Glue is a sticky substance.*

subtract to find the answer to a sum like this $6 - 3 =$

subway a tunnel made under the ground so that people can get to the other side of a road safely

succeed to do or get what you wanted to do or get *She succeeded in winning the race.*

successful able to do or get what you wanted to do or get

such **1** of the same kind *sweets such as these*
2 so great *It was such a surprise!*

suck **1** to take in air or liquid from something *I sucked milk through a straw.*
2 to keep moving something around inside your mouth without chewing it *He sucked a sweet.*

sudden happening quickly without any warning *a sudden scream*

suede (*say* swade)
a kind of soft leather that is not shiny

suet (*say* soo-it)
hard fat that comes from sheep and cattle and is used in cooking

suffer to have to put up with pain or something else that is not pleasant

sufficient enough

sugar a sweet food that is put in drinks and other foods to make them taste sweet

suggest to give someone an idea that you think is useful

suit **1** a jacket and a pair of trousers or skirt that are meant to be worn together
2 to fit in with someone's plans *Does it suit you if we start at once?*
3 to look well on someone *That colour suits you.*

suitable just right for something *suitable shoes for dancing*

suitcase   a kind of box with a lid and a handle for carrying clothes and other things on journeys

suite   (*say* sweet)
a set of furniture

sulk   to stop speaking to your friends, because you are angry about something

sultana   a dried grape

summer   the hottest part of the year

summit   the top of a mountain

sun   the large, round light in the sky that gives the earth heat and light

sundial   a kind of clock that uses a shadow made by the sun to show what time it is

sundial

sung   see **sing**

sunk   see **sink**

sunny   with the sun shining   *a sunny day*

sunrise   the time when the sun rises

sunset   the time when the sun goes down

sunshine   the light and heat that come from the sun when it is shining

supermarket   a large shop where people help themselves to things as they go round and pay for them all on the way out

supersonic   faster than sound travels   *a supersonic aeroplane*

supper   a meal or snack eaten in the evening

supply   1 to give what is needed   *The school supplies all our pencils.*
2 things kept ready to be used when needed   *a supply of paper*

support   1 to hold up something so that it does not fall
2 to give help to someone

suppose   to think something is true although it might not be

sure   knowing something is true or right   *I'm sure her name is Mary.*

surface   1 the part all round the outside of something
2 the top of a table or desk

surgeon   a doctor who is trained to do operations

surgery   the room you go in to see a doctor or dentist

surname   your last name that is the same as your family's name

surprise   1 the feeling you have when something suddenly happens that you were not expecting   *To her surprise, she saw a cow in her garden.*
2 something that happens and was not expected

surrender   to stop fighting and agree to obey the enemy

surround   to be all round someone or something   *The playground is surrounded by a fence.*

suspect   to have a feeling that there might be something wrong

suspicious   feeling that there might be something wrong

swallow   1 to make something go down your throat
2 a bird with a dark blue body, a long tail, and pointed wings

swam   see **swim**

swamp   an area of very wet ground

swan   a big white bird with a very long neck that lives on water or near to it

swap   (*rhymes with* hop) to change one thing for another thing

swarm   a large number of insects together   *a swarm of bees*

sway   to move from side to side

swear   **1** to make a very serious promise   *He has sworn to tell the truth.* **2** to use bad words   *He swore when he hit his finger.*

sweat   to lose liquid through your skin, because you are ill or very hot *He was sweating after running the race.*

sweater   a jersey

sweep   **1** to use a brush to clear away dust and litter from something   *I swept this floor yesterday.* **2** someone whose job is to clean chimneys

sweet   **1** with the taste of sugar or honey **2** very pleasant   *a sweet smell* **3** a small piece of sweet food made of sugar or chocolate   *a bag of sweets* **4** a pudding

swell   to get bigger   *My broken ankle has swollen.*

swallows 2

swelling   a swollen place on the body

swept   see **sweep**

swerve   to move suddenly to one side so that you will not bump into something

swift   **1** quick **2** a bird with long wings that flies very quickly

swift 2

swill   the food and liquid given to pigs

swim   **1** to move the body through water, without touching the bottom *I swam a length yesterday.* **2** to cross water by swimming *She has swum the Channel.*

swindle   to make someone believe something that is not true in order to get something valuable from them

swing   **1** to move backwards and forwards, from side to side, or in a curve   *The door swung open in the wind.* **2** a seat hung from a tree or metal bar so that it can move backwards and forwards

swipe   to hit hard   *He swiped at the ball and it went over the fence.*

swirl   to move around quickly in circles *The water swirled down the drain.*

switch   **1** anything that is turned or pressed in order to make something work or stop working   *an electric light switch* **2** to change from one thing to another *She switched from ballet to tap-dancing.*

swollen   see **swell**

swoop   to fly down suddenly to attack something

sword   (*say* sord)
a weapon like a knife with a very long blade

swore, sworn   see **swear**

swum   see **swim**

swung   see **swing**

sycamore   a kind of large tree. Its seeds have wings and so they can be carried a long way by the wind.

syllable   any word or part of a word that has one separate sound when you say it. *Bi-cy-cle* has three syllables and *bike* has one syllable.

symmetrical   with two halves that are exactly alike but the opposite way round. Butterflies, spectacles, and wheels are symmetrical.

sympathy   the feeling you have when you are sorry for someone who is sad, ill, or in trouble, and want to help them

synagogue   a building where Jews worship

syrup   a very sweet, sticky, liquid

system   a set of parts, things, or ideas that work together   *In London there is an underground railway system.*

T t

tabby   **1** a grey or brown cat with dark stripes in its fur
2 a female cat

table   **1** a piece of furniture with a flat top and legs
2 a list of facts arranged in order

table-cloth   a piece of material spread over a table to cover it

tablet   a small, solid piece of medicine

tack   **1** a short nail with a flat top
2 to sew two pieces of material together quickly, with long stitches

tackle   **1** to try to do a job that needs doing   *We must tackle the mess in the garage.*
2 to try to get the ball from someone else in a football game
3 all the things needed for doing something   *fishing tackle*

tadpole   a tiny creature that lives in water and will turn into a frog, toad, or newt

tail   the part at the end of something. Most animals have tails and so do aeroplanes.

tailor   someone whose job is to make suits and coats

take   **1** to get hold of something   *He took his prize and smiled.*
2 to carry or lead away   *The money was taken yesterday.   Dad is taking us to the zoo.*

take-away   a place where you can buy cooked food to take away

tale   a story

talent   the ability to do something very well   *a talent for singing*

talk   to speak to other people

talkative   fond of talking

tall   measuring more than usual from top to bottom   *a tall person, a tall tree*

tambourine   a musical instrument that you shake or hit with your fingers

tame   not wild or dangerous. Tame animals can be kept as pets, because they are not frightened of people.

tamper   to make changes in something so that it will not work properly

tan   **1** skin that has gone brown because of the sun   *a sun-tan*
2 light brown   *a tan-coloured suitcase*
3 to make the skin of an animal into leather   *The man was tanning the seal skin.*

tangerine   a kind of small orange

tangled   twisted up in knots   *tangled wool, tangled hair*

tank   **1** a large container for liquid. Fish tanks are made of glass and hot water tanks are made of metal.
2 a kind of very strong, heavy car used in war. It has a big gun on top and two long strips of metal round its wheels so that it can move over rough ground.

tanker   **1** a large ship for carrying oil
2 a large lorry for carrying milk or petrol

tanker 1

tanker 2

tape   **1** a narrow strip of cotton used in tying things and making loops or labels for clothes   *name tapes*
2 a narrow strip of special plastic used in a tape-recorder   *cassette tape*

taper   to get very narrow at one end

tape-recorder   a machine for recording on tape and playing it back

tapestry   a piece of strong cloth covered with stitches that make a picture

tar   a thick, black, sticky liquid made from coal or wood and used for making roads

target   something that people aim at and try to hit

tart   **1** pastry with jam or fruit on it
2 very sour. Rhubarb without sugar tastes tart.

tartan   Scottish woollen cloth woven with a check pattern and used for making kilts

tartan

task   a piece of work that must be done

tassel   a bundle of threads tied together at the top and used to decorate things

taste   **1** to eat a little bit of food or sip a drink to see what it is like
2 the flavour something has when you taste it

tasty with a strong, pleasant taste
tasty kippers

tattered badly torn *The slippers were tattered after the puppy chewed them.*

taught see **teach**

tax money that people have to give to the government

taxi a car that you can travel in if you pay the driver *two taxis*

tea **1** a hot drink made with boiling water and the dried leaves of a tea-plant
2 a meal eaten in the afternoon

teach to make someone else able to understand or do something
She taught me to swim last year.

teacher someone whose job is to teach

team a group of people who work together or play together on the same side in a game

teapot a kind of jug with a spout and lid, used for making tea

tear[1] (*rhymes with* fear)
a small drop of water that comes out of the eye when you cry

tear[2] (*rhymes with* fair)
to pull something apart so that you damage it *I tore the letter up and threw it away. His coat was torn.*

tease to bother or annoy someone for fun

teem **1** to rain very hard
2 to be full of moving things *The river was teeming with fish.*

teenager someone who is between thirteen and nineteen years old

teeth more than one tooth

telegraph **1** to send a telemessage
2 *telegraph pole* a tall pole that holds up telephone wires

telemessage a short message that the post office sends very quickly

telephone **1** an instrument that makes sound travel along wires so that you can speak to someone far away
2 to use a telephone to speak to someone

telescope a tube with lenses at each end. People look through telescopes in order to see things that are far away.

telescope

television a machine that picks up programmes sent through the air and changes them into pictures and sound so that people can watch them

tell to speak in order to pass on news, a story, or instructions *I told you about it yesterday.*

temper **1** the mood someone is in
in a good temper in a bad temper
2 *to lose your temper* to become very angry

temperature how hot or cold something is *They measured the temperature in the classroom.*

temple a place where some people worship

temporary for a short time only
They were in a temporary classroom while their own was being decorated.

tempt to try to make someone do wrong
The gang tempted him to steal.

temptation something that makes you want to do wrong   *The money on the desk was a temptation to the thief.*

tend   **1** to be likely to do something   *He tends to fall asleep after dinner.*
2 to look after   *His grandfather tends the allotment.*

tender   **1** loving   *a tender smile*
2 soft   *tender meat*
3 sore   *tender skin*

tennis a game played by two or four people with rackets and a ball on a court with a net across the middle

tent a kind of shelter made of canvas stretched over poles. People sleep in tents when they are camping.

tents

tepid only just warm   *tepid water*

term the time between the main holidays, when school is open. There are three school terms in a year.

terminus a place where a bus or train stops at the end of its journey

terrace   **1** a row of houses that are joined together
2 one of the set of stone steps where people stand to watch football matches   *the terraces*

terrapin a creature that lives in water and looks like a small tortoise

terrible very bad   *terrible weather*

terrier a kind of small dog

terrific   **1** very good   *a terrific idea*
2 very big   *a terrific skyscraper*

terrify to make a person or animal very frightened   *The rabbit was terrified when it saw the fox.*

territory land that belongs to one country or person

terror great fear

test   **1** questions you have to answer to show how good you are at something   *a spelling test*
2 to try out   *Test the brakes.*

tether to tie an animal up so that it has room to move about, but cannot get away

than compared with another person or thing   *You are smaller than me.*

thank to tell someone you are pleased about something they have given you or done for you

thankful wanting to thank someone for what they have done

that the one there   *That is mine, this is yours.   Those books are yours.*

thatch straw or reeds used for covering a roof

thaw   **1** to make ice or snow melt   *She thawed some snow to get water.*
2 the melting of ice or snow   *At last the thaw began.*

terrapin

theatre   a place where people go to see plays and shows

theft   stealing   *the theft of the diamond*

their   belonging to them   *their coats*

them   see **they**

themselves   **1** they and no one else
2 *by themselves*   on their own

then   **1** after that
2 at that time   *We didn't know about it then.*

there   in that place or to that place   *Stand there!*

therefore   and so

thermometer   an instrument that measures temperature   *The thermometer showed how hot it was.*

thermometer

these   see **this**

they   the people or things you are talking about   *They all like cake.*
I gave each of them a sweet.

thick   measuring a lot from one side to the other   *a thick slice of cake*

thicken   **1** to make thicker   *She thickened the gravy with flour.*
2 to get thicker   *The mixture will thicken when you boil it.*

thief   someone who steals things
Ali Baba and the forty thieves

thigh   the top part of the leg down to the knee

thimble   a metal or plastic cover for the end of a finger. You wear it when you sew to protect your finger from the needle.

thin   not fat or thick

thing   anything that can be seen or touched

think   **1** to use your mind
2 to have an idea   *I thought you were wrong.*

third   **1** one of the three equal parts something can be divided into. It can also be written as ⅓.
2 coming after the second   *third prize*

thirst   the feeling that you want to drink.

thirsty   wanting a drink   *After the race she was thirsty.*

this   the one here   *This is mine, that is yours.   These books are mine.*

thistle   a wild plant with prickly leaves and purple flowers

thistle

thorn   a sharp, pointed part on a plant's stem. Roses have thorns.

thorough   **1** done properly and carefully   *thorough work*
2 complete   *a thorough mess*

those   see **that**

though   and yet or although   *It was very cold though it didn't snow.*

thought **1** see **think**
2 something that you think

thoughtful **1** thinking a lot
2 thinking kindly about others and what they would like

thrash to keep hitting someone with a stick

thread **1** a long, thin piece of cotton, nylon, or wool used for sewing or weaving cloth
2 to put thread through the eye of a needle or the hole in a bead

threat a promise that you will do something bad if what you want does not happen

threaten to make threats

thresh to get the seeds out of corn by beating it

threw see **throw**

thrifty careful with money

thrill a sudden excited feeling

thrilling very exciting

throat the front of the neck and the tube inside it that takes foods, liquid, and air into the body

throb to beat heavily. Your heart throbs when you have been running very fast.

throne a special chair for a king or queen

throne

throttle to kill someone by squeezing their throat until they cannot breathe

through from one end or side to the other *We went through the tunnel.*

throughout all through *It was hot throughout the day.*

throw to make something move through the air *He threw a stone and smashed the window. Jonah was thrown into the sea.*

thrush a bird that has a white front with brown spots on it

thrush

thrust to push hard *He thrust his sword into the monster and killed it.*

thud to make the low, dull sound something heavy and large makes when it hits the ground

thumb the short, thick finger at the side of each hand

thump to hit hard with the fist

thunder the loud noise that you hear after a flash of lightning in a storm

thunderstorm a storm with thunder and lightning

tick **1** to make the sound some clocks or watches keep making when they are working
2 a small mark like this √

ticket a piece of paper or card that you buy so that you can travel on a bus or train or get into places like cinemas and theatres

tickle to keep touching part of someone's body lightly with your fingers or a feather. Most people laugh when they are tickled.

tide the movement of the sea towards the land and away from the land

tidy neatly arranged with nothing out of place *a tidy room*

tie 1 to fasten something with a knot or bow *He's tying it up with ribbon.*
2 a long strip of material tied round the collar of a shirt so that the ends hang down the front

tiger a big wild cat found in India and China. It has yellow fur with black stripes.

tiger

tight fitting very closely *tight shoes, a tight lid*

tighten 1 to make tighter *He tightened the screw with the screwdriver.*
2 to get tighter *The rope tightened as the boat moved away.*

tights a piece of clothing that fits closely over the feet, legs, and lower part of the body. Women and girls wear tights. *a pair of tights*

tiles

tile a thin piece of baked clay or something else that is stiff, used in covering a roof, wall, or floor

till 1 until *She waited till the rain had stopped.*
2 a drawer or box for money in a shop *The assistant put the money in the till.*

tilt to make something slope *Don't tilt the table.*

timber wood that can be used for making things

time 1 seconds, minutes, hours, days, weeks, months, and years
2 a certain moment in the day *What time is it? It's time for tea.*
3 the rhythm and speed of a piece of music

timid not brave *The timid mouse hid at the back of the cage.*

tingle to sting a little bit *Her ears were tingling with the cold.*

tinkle to make the light, ringing sound a small bell makes

tinsel thin, shiny, silver ribbon. Tinsel is used for decorating things at Christmas.

tiny very small

tip 1 the part right at the end of something
2 a small gift of money given to someone for their help
3 a place where rubbish is left
4 to turn something over so that the things inside it fall out

tiptoe to walk on your toes without making a sound *She tiptoed away.*

tired 1 needing to rest or sleep 2 bored with something *I'm tired of work.*

tissue very thin, soft paper

title 1 the name of a book, film, picture, or piece of music 2 a word like Sir, Lady, Dr., Mr., and Mrs. that is put in front of a person's name

titter to laugh in a silly way

toad

toad an animal like a big frog. It has rough, dry skin and lives on land.

toadstool a plant that looks like a mushroom. Most toadstools are poisonous.

toast bread cooked until it is crisp and brown *beans on toast*

tobacco a plant with leaves that are dried and smoked in pipes or used to make cigars and cigarettes

toboggan a kind of sledge used for sliding down slopes covered in snow

today this day

toddler a young child just beginning to walk

toe one of the five separate parts at the end of each foot

toffee butter and sugar cooked together and made into sticky sweets

together 1 with another *joined together* 2 at the same time as another *They sang together.*

toil to do hard work

toilet a lavatory

token a round piece of plastic or a kind of ticket, used instead of money to pay for something *bus tokens, record tokens*

told see **tell**

tomahawk an axe once used by American Indians

tomato a soft, round, red fruit with seeds inside it. Tomatoes are eaten raw in salads.

tomb (*rhymes with* room) a place where a dead person's body is buried. Some tombs are above the ground.

tomorrow the day after today

ton a large measure for weight

tone 1 a musical sound 2 the kind of sound someone's voice has *a gentle tone*

tongs

tongs a tool used for getting hold of something and picking it up

tongue the long, soft, pink part that moves about inside the mouth

tonight this evening or night

tonne a large measure for weight
1 tonne = 1000 Kilograms

tonsils parts of the throat that
sometimes cause an illness called
tonsillitis

too **1** as well *Can I come too?*
2 more than is needed *too much*

took see take

tool something that you use to help you
to do a job. Hammers and saws are
tools.

tooth one of the hard, white parts in the
mouth *Brush your teeth after every
meal.*

toothache a pain in a tooth

toothbrush a small brush with a long
handle, for cleaning teeth

toothpaste a thick paste put on a
toothbrush and used for cleaning teeth

topic something interesting that you are
writing or talking about

topple to fall over because there is too
much on top

topsy-turvy turned upside-down

torch an electric light that you can carry
about with you

torch

tore see tear²

torment to keep bothering or annoying
someone or something for fun,
although it is cruel

torn see tear²

torpedo a kind of long, round bomb
sent under water to destroy ships and
submarines *two torpedoes*

torrent a very fast stream of water

tortoise a creature with four legs and a
shell over its body, that moves slowly

tortoise

torture **1** great pain that seems as if it
will never end *The pain of the
toothache was torture.*
2 to make someone feel great pain
*The bully tortured the little animal by
tying up its legs.*

toss to throw into the air

total the amount when you have added
everything up

totter to walk very shakily as if you are
going to fall over. Young children totter
when they are learning to walk.

touch **1** to feel something with part of
your body
2 to be so close to something else that
there is no space in between

tough **1** strong *tough shoes, a tough
fighter*
2 hard to chew *tough meat*

tour **1** a journey you make to visit
different places
2 to walk round a place looking at
different things

tow to pull along with a rope or chain

toward, towards in the direction of something *He walked towards the school.*

towel a piece of cloth for drying things that are wet *a bath towel, a tea towel*

tower **1** a tall, narrow building *Blackpool Tower*
2 a tall, narrow part of a building *a church tower*

town a place with schools, shops, offices, factories, and a lot of houses built near each other

towpath a path beside a canal or river

toy something you play with

trace **1** a mark left by something
2 to copy a picture using thin paper that you can see through. You put the paper over the picture and follow its lines with a pencil.

track **1** a kind of path
2 a railway line
3 to follow the marks left by a person or animal

tractor a machine with wheels and an engine that is used on farms to pull heavy things

tragedy **1** something very sad that has happened *It was a tragedy that the dog was run over.*
2 a play with a very sad ending

trail **1** a rough path
2 smells and marks left behind by an animal. People follow trails when they are hunting.
3 to be dragged along the ground *Your scarf is trailing in the mud.*

trailer something that is pulled along by a car or lorry

train **1** railway coaches joined together and pulled by an engine
2 to teach a person or animal how to do something
3 to practise for a competition or game

traitor someone who gives away a secret or gives information about their friends or country to the enemy

tramp **1** someone without a home or job who walks from place to place
2 to walk heavily

trample to spoil something by walking heavily on it *The clumsy cattle trampled on the flowers.*

trampoline a large piece of canvas joined to a metal frame with springs for bouncing up and down on

tractor

trampoline

trade buying and selling *Our country does a lot of trade with other countries.*

traffic cars, buses, bicycles, lorries, and other things travelling on the road

trance   a kind of sleep

transfer   to move someone or something to another place   *He was transferred to a different team.*

transform   to make a great change in a person or thing   *The caterpillar is transformed into a butterfly.*

transistor radio   a kind of radio that you can carry about with you easily

transparent   so clear that you can see through it. Glass is transparent.

transport   to take people, animals, or things from one place to another

trap   **1** something made for catching an animal and keeping it prisoner
2 to catch a person or animal by using a trap or a clever trick   *They trapped the mouse by using cheese as bait.*

trapdoor   a kind of door in the floor or ceiling

trapeze   a bar hanging from ropes, used by acrobats

travel   to go from one place to another

trawler   a fishing boat that pulls a large net along the bottom of the sea

tray   a flat piece of wood or tin used for carrying food, cups, plates, and other light things

treacherous   not to be trusted   *The treacherous guard killed the king.*

tricycle

treacle   a thick, sweet, sticky liquid. Treacle is eaten on bread and used in making cakes and puddings.

tread   to walk on something   *He trod on his glasses and broke them.*

treason   giving away your country's secrets to the enemy

treasure   gold, silver, jewels, or other valuable things

treat   **1** to behave towards someone or something in a certain way   *The horse had been badly treated.*
2 to pay for another person's food or drink   *My uncle treated us to lunch in a restaurant.*
3 something special that pleases you very much   *a birthday treat*

tree   any tall plant with leaves, branches, and a thick stem of wood

tremble   to shake because you are cold or frightened

tremendous   very large or great

trench   a long, narrow hole dug in the ground

trespass   to go on someone else's land, without asking them if you can

trial   **1** trying something out to see how well it works
2 the time when a prisoner is in court. The people there decide whether or not he has done something wrong.

triangle   a flat shape with three straight edges and three corners

tribe   a group of families who live together and are ruled by a chief

trick   **1** something very clever that a person or animal has learnt to do
2 to make someone believe something that is not true

trickle   to move like a very small stream of water

tricycle   a machine with three wheels and two pedals that is ridden

tried see **try**

trifle cake and fruit covered in jelly, custard, and cream

trigger the part of a gun that is pulled to fire it

trim **1** to cut away the extra parts of something to make it neat and tidy
2 to decorate a piece of clothing *a coat trimmed with fur*

trio a set of three people or things

trip **1** a short journey *a school trip*
2 to fall over something *I tripped over and broke my leg.*

triumphant very pleased because you have been successful *a triumphant smile*

trod, trodden see **tread**

trolley **1** a small, narrow table on wheels
2 a kind of basket on wheels used in supermarkets

troop an organized group of soldiers or Scouts

tropical belonging to the very hot countries in Africa, Asia, and South America *tropical plants*

trot one of the ways a horse can move. It is faster than a walk but slower than a canter.

trouble **1** something that upsets, worries, or bothers you
2 *to take trouble over something* to take great care when you are doing something

trough (*say* troff)
a long, narrow container that holds food or water for farm animals *a pig trough, a horse trough*

trousers a piece of clothing that covers the body from the waist to the ankles and has separate parts for the legs *a pair of trousers*

trout

trout a fish found in rivers and lakes

trowel a small spade with a short handle

truant a pupil who stays away from school without permission

truck **1** a kind of lorry
2 a cart pulled by a railway engine, for carrying things

trudge to walk slowly and heavily because you are tired

true correct or real *a true story, a true friend*

truly in a true or honest way

trumpet a brass musical instrument that is blown

trumpet

trunk **1** a tree's thick stem
2 an elephant's long nose
3 a large box with a lid and handle for carrying things on a journey or storing things

trust to believe that someone or something will not let you down

truth   something that is true

try   **1** to work at something you want to be able to do
2 to test something   *I tried it out before I bought it.*

tub   a round container   *a tub of ice cream*

tube   **1** a long, thin, round container   *a tube of toothpaste*
2 a long, thin, hollow piece of plastic, rubber, glass, or metal. Tubes are used for taking water and gas from one place to another.

tuck   **1** to tidy away the loose ends of something   *She tucked her blouse into her skirt.*
2 *tucked up*   warm and comfortable in bed

tuft   a number of feathers, hairs, or blades of grass growing together

tug   **1** to pull hard   *He tugged at the rope and broke it.*
2 a boat used for pulling ships

tulip   a spring flower that grows from a bulb and is shaped like a cup

tumble   to fall

tumbler   a glass with a flat bottom   *a tumbler of water*

tune   a series of notes that make a piece of music   *Listen to the tune and then try to sing it yourself.*

tunic   **1** a dress worn over a shirt
2 a kind of long jacket worn as part of a uniform   *The soldier's tunic had medals pinned on it.*

tunnel   a long hole that has been made under the ground or through a hill

turban   a covering for the head made by wrapping cloth around it in a special way

turbine   a kind of engine with a wheel inside it turned by gas, water, or steam

turf   short grass and the soil it is growing in

turkey   a large bird kept for its meat

turn   **1** to move round
2 to change   *The prince turned into a frog.*
3 to become   *She turned pale.*
4 a time for you to do something that the others have done or are still waiting to do   *It's his turn to set the table.*

turnip   a round, white vegetable eaten in the winter

turntable   the part of a record-player that you put the record on

turpentine   a kind of oil that can be used for cleaning paint brushes and mixed with paint to make it thinner

turret   a small tower in a castle

turtle   a sea creature that looks like a tortoise

turtle

turbine

typewriter

tusk one of the two long, pointed teeth an elephant has

tweed warm cloth woven from wool *a tweed coat*

tweezers a small tool for getting hold of very thin things such as stamps *a pair of tweezers*

twice two times

twig a small, thin branch

twilight the dim light at the end of the day before it gets completely dark

twin one of two children born to the same mother at the same time

twine thin, strong string

twinkle to shine with a lot of tiny flashes of bright light. Stars twinkle.

twirl to turn round and round quickly

twist 1 to turn or bend *a twisted ankle* 2 to wrap things round each other

twitch to keep making quick movements with part of the body. Rabbits twitch their noses.

twitter to keep making quick, light sounds like a bird

type 1 one kind or sort *That bird is a type of duck.* 2 to write with a typewriter *He typed a letter.*

typewriter a machine with keys that you press in order to print letters and numbers

tyre a circle of rubber round the rim of a wheel

U u

ugly not pleasant to look at *the ugly sisters*

umbrella a round piece of cloth stretched over a frame that can be opened and shut. You hold an umbrella over your head to keep off the rain.

umpire someone who makes sure that the rules are kept in games such as cricket and tennis

uncle your aunt's husband or the brother of one of your parents

uncomfortable not comfortable *Her tight shoes hurt her feet and were very uncomfortable.*

unconscious (*say un-kon-shuss*) *in a very deep sleep After the accident he was unconscious for a week.*

under below

underground 1 under the ground 2 a railway that runs through tunnels under the ground *the London Underground*

undergrowth bushes and other plants growing under tall trees

underline to draw a straight line underneath a word

underneath in a place under something

understand to know what something means or how it works *He understood what the Frenchman said.*

underwear clothes made to be worn under other clothes

undo to open something that has been fastened with a knot or a button   *I undid the knot and opened the parcel. Your shoe is undone.*

undress to take clothes off

unemployment when there are not enough jobs for the people who want to work

uneven not smooth or level

unexpected not expected   *I had an unexpected letter from an old friend.*

unfair not right or just   *an unfair game*

ungrateful not grateful   *The ungrateful child never thanked them for the present.*

unhappy not happy

unhealthy not healthy

unicorn an imaginary animal. It is like a horse, but has a long, straight horn growing out of the front of its head.

unicorn

uniform the special clothes that everyone in a group wears so that they look smart together   *a school uniform*

union a group of workers who have joined together to make sure that everyone is treated fairly by the people in charge

unique very unusual because it is the only one of its kind   *a unique painting*

unit **1** the number one   *hundreds, tens, and units*
2 an amount used in measuring or counting. Centimetres are units of length and pence are units of money.

unite to join together to make one

universal having to do with everyone and everything

universe all the worlds that there are and everyone and everything in them

university a place where some people go to study when they have left school

unkind not kind

unless if not

unlike not like

unload **1** to take off the things that an animal, boat, car, or lorry is carrying   *They unloaded the ship at the dock.*
2 to take the bullets out of a gun

unlock to open a door or box with a key

unlucky not lucky

unnecessary not necessary   *It is unnecessary to wear your glasses when you're asleep.*

unpleasant not pleasant   *The smell of the rubbish was most unpleasant.*

unruly badly behaved and difficult to control

untidy not tidy

until up to a certain time   *I stayed up until midnight.*

unusual not usual

unwell ill

unwrap to take something out of the paper it is wrapped in

upon on or on top of

upper higher   *the upper lip*

upright **1** standing straight up   *an upright post*
2 honest   *an upright person*

uproar loud noise made by people who are angry or excited about something

upset 1 to make someone unhappy 2 to knock over *I upset the pot and spilt the paint.*

upside-down turned over so that the bottom is at the top

upstairs the part of a house that you get to by climbing the stairs

upward, upwards moving to somewhere higher

urge 1 to try to make someone hurry to do something 2 a sudden, strong wish to do something *On the mountain he had an urge to fly like a bird.*

urgent so important that it needs to be answered or done at once *an urgent message, urgent work*

use to do a job with something *I used paper and glue to make it.*

useful 1 able to be used a lot *a useful tool* 2 helpful *useful information*

useless not useful *A car is useless without petrol.*

usual happening most often *Dinner is at the usual time.*

utensil any tool, pot, or pan used in the kitchen

V v

vacant with nobody in it *a vacant room*

vaccination (*say* vak-si-nation) an injection that stops you getting an illness

vacuum cleaner a machine that sucks up dust and dirt from floors and carpets

vague not clear or certain *a vague idea*

vain 1 too proud of yourself and how you look 2 *in vain* without success *They tried in vain to save his life.*

valley low land between hills

valuable worth a lot of money *valuable jewellery*

value 1 the amount of money something could be sold for 2 how important or useful something is

valve a part in a machine that makes air, liquid, or electricity go in only one direction

vanilla the flavour that white ice cream has

vanish to go away suddenly and not be seen any more

vanity being too proud of yourself

vapour steam, mist, or smoke are all vapours. Other vapours are invisible.

variety 1 a lot of different kinds of things *a variety of flavours* 2 a certain sort *That shop sells twenty varieties of ice-cream.*

various different

varnish a clear liquid painted on to wood or metal to make it shiny

vary to be different *varied colours*

vacuum cleaner

vase a jar for holding flowers

vast very large

veal meat from a calf

vegetable part of a plant used as food. Vegetables are usually eaten with the main part of a meal.

vegetarian (*say* vej-et-air-ee-an) a person who does not eat meat

vehicle anything that takes people or things from one place to another on land. Cars, vans, buses, bicycles, trains, carts, and lorries are all vehicles.

veil a piece of thin material used to cover the face or head

vein one of the narrow tubes inside the body, that carry blood to the heart

velvet thick material that is smooth and soft on one side *a velvet dress*

venom the poison of snakes

ventilator a kind of opening in the wall of a room for letting in fresh air

veranda a long, open place with a roof built on to the side of a house

veranda

veranda

verb any of the words that tell you what someone or something is doing. *Come, go, sit, eat, sleep,* and *think* are all verbs.

verge grass growing along the edge of a road or path

verse part of a poem or song

version a story about something that has happened *His version of the accident is different from mine.*

vertical upright *You can't climb that cliff – it's almost vertical!*

very most *Ice is very cold.*

vessel any container for liquid

vest a piece of underwear worn on the top half of the body

vet someone whose job is to help animals that are ill or hurt to get better

viaduct a long bridge that is a row of arches with a railway or road along the top of it

vicar someone who serves God by being in charge of a church

vicious (*say* vish-uss) bad and cruel *a vicious kick, a vicious temper*

victim someone who has been hurt, robbed, or killed

victory the winning of a fight or game

video the recording on special tape of pictures and sound to be played on a television screen

video game an electronic game which is played on a television screen

video recorder a machine that uses special tape to make copies of television programmes so that they can be watched again later

video recorder

view 1 everything that can be seen from one place
2 what a person thinks about something   *My view is that school holidays are too short.*

vigour   strength

vile   very nasty   *a vile smell*

village   a group of houses together with a church and other buildings, in the country

villain   a bad man

vine   a plant that bunches of grapes grow on

vinegar   a sour liquid put on food to make it taste better. People put salt and vinegar on chips.

violent   very strong and rough   *a violent storm*

violet 1 a tiny purple or white flower that grows in spring
2 purple

violin   a musical instrument made of wood with strings across it that are played with a bow

violin

visibility   how clearly something can be seen. In fog visibility is poor.

visible   able to be seen

vision 1 the ability to see   *Glasses will improve your vision.*
2 a kind of dream   *He saw things in a vision and he thought they were real.*

visitor   someone who goes to see a person or place

vivid 1 bright   *vivid colours*
2 lively   *a vivid imagination*
3 so clear it seems real   *a vivid dream*

vixen   a female fox

vocabulary   a list of the words someone uses

voice   the sound you make with your mouth when you are speaking or singing

volcano   a mountain that contains hot liquid, gases, and ash that sometimes burst out of it
two volcanoes

volcano

volume 1 the amount of space filled by something.
The volume of something is its length × its breadth × its height.
2 one of a set of books   *The encyclopedia has ten volumes.*
3 how loud a sound is   *Turn down the volume on your radio.*

volunteer   someone who offers to do something that they do not have to do

vote   to say which person or idea you think should be chosen. Sometimes people vote by putting up their hands and sometimes by making a mark on a piece of paper.

voucher   a printed paper you can use instead of money for buying certain things   *a gift voucher*

vow   to make a serious promise   *The Cub Scouts made a vow to do their best.*

vowel   any one of the letters, a, e, i, o, u, and sometimes y

voyage   a long journey by boat

vulture   a large bird that eats dead animals

W w

waddle   to walk like a duck. Ducks take very short steps and move their bodies from side to side.

wade   to walk through water

wafer   a very thin biscuit. Ice cream often has wafers with it.

wag   to move quickly from side to side   *The dog wagged its tail.*

wage, wages   the money paid to someone for the job they do

wagon   a cart with four wheels that is pulled by horses and used for moving heavy things

wail   to make a long, sad cry

waist   the narrow part in the middle of the body

waistcoat   a short jacket without sleeves or a collar

wait   to stay for something that you are expecting to happen

waiter   a man who brings food to people in cafés, hotels, and restaurants

waitress   a woman who brings food to people in cafés, hotels, and restaurants

wake   to stop sleeping   *Wake up! He woke suddenly and saw the thief. I was woken by the noise.*

walk   to move along on foot

walkie-talkie   a kind of radio that is carried about and can be used like a telephone

walkie-talkies

wall   **1** a barrier made of bricks or stone put round a garden or field   **2** one of the sides of a building or room

wallet   a small, flat, leather case for money and papers that is carried in the pocket

walnut   a kind of nut with a hard shell

waltz   a kind of dance done with a partner

wand   a thin stick used for casting magic spells. In stories fairies and wizards have wands.

wander   to move about without trying to get anywhere   *They wandered in the wood picking flowers.*

want   **1** to feel that you would like to have something   *I want a new coat.*   **2** to need   *That car wants washing.*

war   a fight between countries

ward   a bedroom for patients in a hospital

wardrobe   a cupboard where clothes are hung

warehouse   a large building in which things are stored

warm   fairly hot   *a warm room*

warn   to tell someone that they are in danger

warren   an area of ground where a lot of rabbits live

warrior   someone fighting in a battle

wart   a dry, hard spot on the skin

wash   to make something clean with water

washing   clothes that need washing or are being washed

washing-machine   a machine that washes clothes

wasp   an insect that flies and can sting

wasp

waste   **1** to use more of something than you need to
2 things that you get rid of because you do not need them any more   *waste paper*

watch   **1** to look at
2 a small clock that is worn or carried

watchman   someone whose job is to guard a building at night

water   the clear liquid in rivers and seas. It falls from the sky as rain.

waterfall   a stream of water falling from a high place to a low place

waterproof   made of material that does not let water through   *a waterproof coat*

watertight   made so that water cannot get into it   *watertight boots*

wave   **1** one of the lines of water you can see moving on the surface of the sea
2 to move your hand to say hello or goodbye to someone   *Look, she's waving to you.*
3 to move up and down or from side to side   *The branches waved in the wind.*

wavy   with curves in it   *wavy hair, a wavy line*

wax   something that melts very easily and is used for making candles, crayons, and polish. Some wax is made by bees and some is made from oil.

way   **1** a road or path   *This is the way to the beach.*
2 how something is done   *This is the way to plait hair.*

weak   not strong   *a weak person, weak tea*

weaken   **1** to get weaker   *The sick bird weakened each day.*
2 to make weaker   *Put more water in the squash if you want to weaken it.*

wealth   a lot of money or treasure

wealthy   rich

weapon   something used to hurt another person in a fight

wear   **1** to be dressed in something   *I wore that dress last time.*
2 to wear out to become weak and useless because it has been used so much
3 to wear someone out to make someone very tired   *He was worn out after the match.*

weary   very tired

weasel   a small, furry animal with a long body. It kills and eats mice, rats, and rabbits.

weather   rain, snow, ice, fog, wind, and sun

weave to make material by pushing a thread under and over other threads *She made a loom and wove a scarf on it. The bag was woven in straw.*

web a thin, sticky net spun by a spider to trap insects

web-foot a foot with its toes joined together by skin. Ducks, otters, and other animals that swim a lot have web-feet.

web-foot

web-foot

wedding the time when a man and woman get married

wedge to keep two things apart by pushing something between them

weed any wild plant that grows where it is not wanted

week the seven days from Sunday to the next Saturday

weekend Saturday and Sunday

weep to let tears fall from the eyes *He wept because he was lost.*

weigh 1 to find the weight of something *She weighed the apples in the scales.*
2 to have a certain weight *What does that bag of potatoes weigh?*

weight 1 how heavy something is *What is your weight?*
2 a round piece of metal put on the scales when something is being weighed *Put the 2lb weight on the scales.*

weird (*rhymes with* beard) very strange

welcome to show that you are pleased when someone or something arrives

welfare the health and happiness of people *The doctor was interested in the welfare of his patients.*

well 1 healthy
2 in a good way *He swims well.*
3 a hole dug to get water or oil out of the ground

wellingtons rubber boots that keep the feet and part of the legs dry *a pair of wellingtons*

went see **go**

wept see **weep**

west in the direction of the setting sun

western 1 from the west or in the west
2 a cowboy film

whack to hit hard with a stick

whale the largest sea animal there is

whale

wharf a place where ships are loaded and unloaded

what 1 which thing *What is that?*
2 that which *Tell me what you think.*

whatever no matter what *Whatever happens, I'll help you.*

wheat a plant grown by farmers. Its seed is used for making flour.

wheel **1** a circle of wood or metal fixed in the middle so that it can keep turning round. Cars, bicycles, carts, and some machines have wheels.
2 to push a bicycle, pram, or cart
Do not cycle here, wheel your bike instead.

wheelbarrow a small cart with one wheel at the front, that is pushed

wheelbarrow

when **1** at what time *When are you coming?*
2 at the time that *When I moved, it flew away.*

whenever at any time

where in what place *Where are you?*

wherever no matter where *Wherever you are, I'll find you.*

whether if *She asked whether I could come.*

which what person or thing *Which do you want?*

while in the time that something else is happening *He fell asleep while the television was on.*

whimper the soft sound an animal makes when it is frightened or hurt

whine the long, sad sound a dog makes when it is unhappy

whip **1** a long piece of rope or leather joined to a handle and used for hitting things
2 to stir cream hard to make it thick *whipped cream*

whirl to turn round and round very quickly

whisk **1** to move very quickly *The nurse whisked away the bandage.*
2 to stir hard *He whisked the cake mixture.*

whisker a strong hair that grows on the faces of men and animals. A cat has long whiskers growing at each side of its mouth.

whisky a drink for adults which uses corn or potatoes to make alcohol

whisper to speak very softly

whistle **1** to make a shrill sound by blowing through the lips
2 something that makes a shrill sound when it is blown

Whit Sunday the seventh Sunday after Easter. It is also called **Whitsun**.

who what person *Who did that?*

whoever no matter what person *Whoever did it will be in trouble.*

whole **1** not broken *Swallow it whole.*
2 all of something *the whole world*

whooping-cough (*say* hooping cough)
an illness that makes you keep coughing and breathing in heavily

whose belonging to what person *Whose is this?*

why because of what *Why did you do that?*

wick the string that goes through the middle of a candle, which you light

wicked very bad *a wicked witch*

wicket   the set of three stumps with two bails on top of them in cricket

bails

wicket

stumps

wide   **1** measuring a lot from one side to the other
2 completely   *wide awake, wide open*

widow   a woman whose husband has died

widower   a man whose wife has died

width   how wide something is

wife   a woman married to someone   *Henry VIII had six wives.*

wig   a covering of false hair worn on the head

wigwam   the kind of tent American Indians used to live in

wild   **1** not looked after by people   la wild flower
2 not controlled   *a wild horse, a wild temper*

wilderness   wild land where no one lives

wilful   wanting to do something, even though other people say it is wrong   *a wilful child*

will   **1** instructions left by a person who has died telling people what they want to be done with their money and things
2 the power to choose what you want to do
3 is going to   *He will be nine tomorrow.   We'll soon be there.
I said I would be late.   I'd like another cake.*

willing   ready and happy to do what is wanted

willow   a kind of tree that grows near water and has thin branches that bend easily. Its wood is used for making cricket bats.

wily   crafty

win   **1** to get a prize
2 to beat someone else in a game or fight   *We've won four matches and lost two.*

wince   to move slightly because you are upset or in pain

wind[1]   (*rhymes with* grinned)
air moving along quickly

wind[2]   (*rhymes with* blind)
1 to turn a key to make a machine work   *The clock started when she wound it up.*
2 to wrap cloth, thread, tape, or string tightly round something

windmill   a mill that uses wind to make its machinery work.

window   an opening in the wall of a building. It is filled with glass and lets in light.

wine   a strong drink make from grapes

wing   one of the parts of a bird or insect used for flying   *a pair of wings*

wink   to close and open one eye quickly

winter   the coldest part of the year

wipe   to rub something with a cloth to dry it or clean it

wire a long, thin strip of metal that can be bent into different shapes

wireless a radio

wisdom the ability to understand many things *They say you gain wisdom as you get older.*

wise able to understand many things

wish to say or think what you would like to happen

wisp a little bit of straw, hair, or smoke

witch a woman who uses magic. Witches in fairy stories have tall, black, pointed hats and ride in the air on brooms.

with **1** having *a man with a wooden leg*
2 in the company of *I came with a friend.*
3 using *It was written with a pen.*
4 against *fighting with the enemy*

wither to dry up and get paler and smaller *withered flowers*

without not having *without any money*

witness someone who sees something important happen *She was a witness to the accident.*

witty clever and funny

windmill

wives more than one wife

wizard a man in fairy stories, who can do magic things

wobble to shake or rock. Jelly wobbles.

woke, woken see **wake**

wolf a wild animal like a big, fierce dog *a pack of wolves*

wolves

woman a fully grown female *The three women were sisters.*

won see **win**

wonder **1** a feeling of surprise because of something strange or marvellous
2 to ask yourself about something *I wonder who did it.*

wonderful so good that it surprises you *a wonderful holiday*

wood **1** the branches and trunks of trees cut up so that they can be used for making things or burnt on fires
2 a lot of trees growing together

wooden made of wood

woodpecker a bird that eats insects living in tree trunks. It has a strong beak for making holes in wood and a long, sticky tongue for catching insects.

woodwork making things out of wood *a woodwork lesson*

wool the thick, soft hair that covers sheep. It is spun into thread and used for making cloth and for knitting.

woollen   made of wool

word   a sound or group of sounds that means something when you say it, write it, or read it

word-processor   a computer with a keyboard and a display screen. It will store and display the words that are typed into it from the keyboard.

wore   see **wear**

work   a job or something else that you have to do

workman   a man paid to work with his hands, a tool, or a machine

workshop   a place where things are made or mended

workshop

world   the earth or anything else in space that is like it

worm   a long, thin creature that wriggles about in the soil

worn   see **wear**

worry   **1** to be upset because you are thinking about something bad that might happen
2 to get hold of something with the teeth and shake it, as dogs do with slippers

worse   less good   *He's a worse swimmer than I am.*

worship   to love and praise someone   *Christians worship God.*

worst   least good   *He's the worst in the class at swimming.*

worth   with a certain value   *This old stamp is worth £100.*

worthless   not worth anything

would   see **will**

wound[1]   (*say* woond)
an injury from something like a knife or a bullet

wound[2]   (*rhymes with* sound)
see **wind**[2]

wove, woven   see **weave**

wrap   to put cloth or paper round something

wreath   flowers or leaves twisted together into a ring   *a holly wreath*

wreck   **1** to damage a ship, building, or car so badly that it cannot be used again   *The earthquake wrecked the building.*
2 a ship, building, or car so badly damaged that it cannot be used again   *The car was a wreck after the accident.*

wren   a very small, brown bird

wrestle   to struggle with someone

wretched   (*say* retch-id)
1 unhappy or ill
2 poor   *wretched health*

wriggle   to twist and turn the body about like a worm

wring   to squeeze and twist something wet to get the water out of it

wrinkle   a small crease in the skin. Old people usually have a lot of wrinkles.

wrist   the thin part of the arm where it is joined to the hand

write   to put words or signs on paper so that people can read them   *I wrote to her last week.*

writhe   to twist or roll about because you are in great pain   *The injured dog was writhing in pain and distress.*

writing   something that has been written   *untidy writing   a piece of writing*

written   see write

wrong   not right   *the wrong answer*

wrote   see write

wrung   see wring

X x

X-ray   a special photograph that shows the inside of a body so that doctors can see if there is anything wrong

X-ray

xylophone   a row of wooden or metal bars that you hit with small hammers to make musical sounds

Y y

yacht   (*say* yot) a light boat with sails, used for racing

yard   **1** a measure for length   **2** ground that is next to a building and has a wall round it

yawn   to open your mouth wide because you are tired

year   a measure for time. A year is twelve months, or three hundred and sixty-five days.

yell   to shout

yelp   to give a quick, shrill cry like a dog in pain

yesterday   the day before today

yew   a kind of tree that has dark green leaves it keeps all through the year

yield   **1** to give in   **2** the amount of fruit or grain on a plant   *a good yield of apples*

yodel   to shout with a musical sound, changing from a low note to a high note and back again

yoghurt   a thick liquid made from sour milk. It usually has fruit in it and you eat it with a spoon.

yolk   (*rhymes with* joke) the round, yellow part of an egg

you   the person or people you are speaking to

young   born not long ago. A kitten is a young cat.

youngster   someone who is young

your   belonging to you   *your book*

yourself, yourselves   **1** you and no one else   **2** *by yourself, by yourselves* on your own

youth   **1** a boy or young man   **2** the time in your life when you are young

Z z

zebra   an animal like a horse with black and white stripes. Zebras are found in Africa.

zero the number nothing, also written 0

zigzag a line with sudden turns in it like this

zip, zipper a special fastener for joining two edges of material together. Some dresses, trousers, and bags have zips.

zone a part of a town, country, or the world that is special in some way *a parking zone*

zoo a place where different kinds of wild animals are kept so that people can go and see them

zoom to move very quickly

zip

Picture Section

ships and boats

deck

stern

funnel

bridge

cable

propeller

keel

lifeboat

porthole

bow

anchor

yacht

mast

sail

helm

cabin

rudder

keel

hull

canoe

kayak

rowing-boat

parts of the body

shoulder
hair
forehead
chest
eyebrow
armpit
elbow
stomach
waist
arm
hip
eyelashes
eye
nose
nostril
ear
wrist
lips
hand
cheek
knuckle
finger
thigh
neck
chin
knee
throat
calf
shin
ankle
toe
heel

fruits

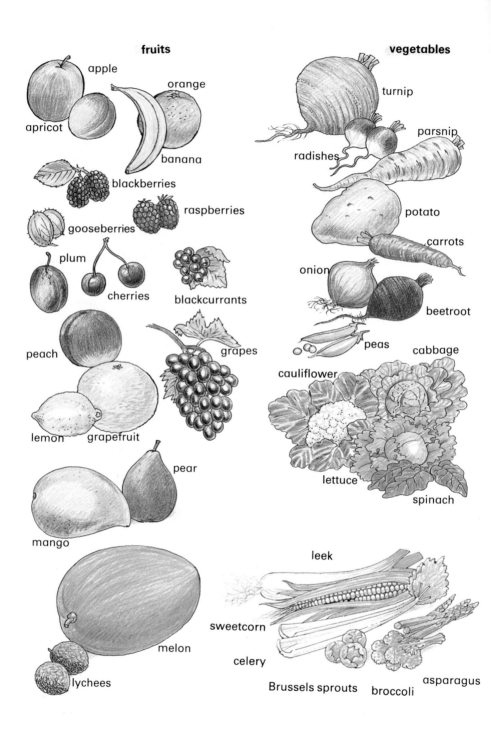

apple

apricot

orange

banana

blackberries

raspberries

gooseberries

plum

cherries

blackcurrants

peach

grapes

lemon   grapefruit

pear

mango

melon

lychees

vegetables

turnip

parsnip

radishes

potato

carrots

onion

beetroot

peas   cabbage

cauliflower

lettuce

spinach

leek

sweetcorn

celery

Brussels sprouts   broccoli   asparagus

flowers and plants

cereals

oats

carnation

dandelion

cowslip

barley

wheat

daffodil

rye   maize

buttercup

daisy

crocus

rose

lily

geranium

cactus

pansy

heather

petal

bluebell

nettle

moss

snowdrop   stalk

trees

leaf

acorn

conker

oak

horse-chestnut

trunk

willow

catkin

beech

poplar

ash

sycamore

cypress

maple

yew

eucalyptus

birch

elm

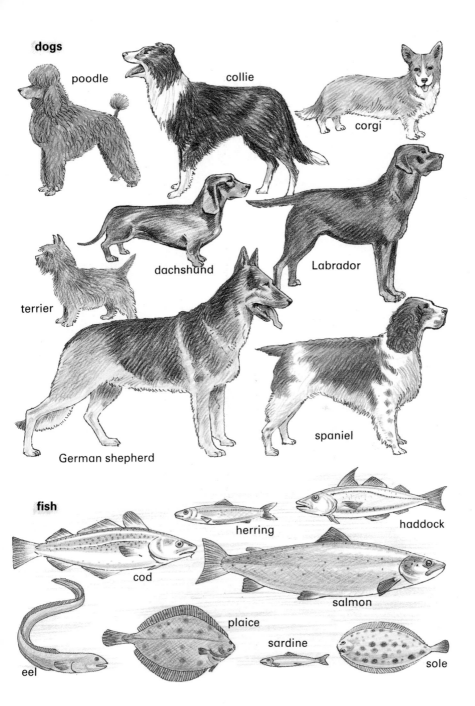

dogs

poodle

collie

corgi

dachshund

Labrador

terrier

German shepherd

spaniel

fish

herring

haddock

cod

salmon

eel

plaice

sardine

sole

musical instruments

violin
cello
double-bass
French horn
trumpet
trombone
tuba
piccolo
oboe
flute
clarinet
piano
bassoon
tambourine
triangle and beater
cymbals